How I
got my postgraduate
degree part time

How I
got my postgraduate degree part time

Edited by
Nicole Greenfield

The Independent Studies How I... Series

School of Independent Studies
Lonsdale College
Lancaster University
Lancaster LA1 4YN

*First published in 2000 by the School of
Independent Studies, Lonsdale College
Lancaster University, Lancaster LA1 4YN*

ISBN 1-86220-091-2

PRINTED ON
RECYCLED PAPER

*Cover design by Rowland & Hird, Lancaster
Printed in Great Britain by
South Ribble Printing Limited
Preston, Lancashire*

Preface by the Series Editor

'The 21st Century has marked the transformation of Britain's 'elite' universities and colleges into a system of mass higher education. This broadening of access has led to a massive expansion in student numbers. Never before has it been so important to understand life at today's higher education establishments - establishments which are too frequently presented in outdated stereotypes.

We are looking for first-hand accounts of both modern and traditional university and college life. Issues such as age, class, gender, race; success and failure; finance, teaching, social life and combining studies with other responsibilities, are all of interest. Appreciation of these issues is not only crucial for those wishing to make the most of their higher education, but also for the success of the staff providing it.

If you are, or are about to be, involved in higher education - as a student, lecturer, research worker or other member of staff - we invite you to analyse and describe your experiences of higher education for publication in this series.'

John Wakeford

Acknowledgements

We would like to thank *The Guardian* for their generous and collaborative support. Through their endorsement of the Independent Studies Series, and their assistance with promotional advertising, we are able to further develop the contributions we are making towards greater understanding of, and improvements to, modern university life.

In particular, we are grateful to Donald Macleod and Gerry O'Connor of *The Guardian* newspaper, for their support of the Series and for their recognition of the significance of these developments.

Nicole Greenfield
Publications Editor

Contents

Introduction
Nicole Greenfield

Part-time study for a higher degree has become the fastest growing sector of Higher Education. Funding is becoming ever more elusive, and the financial strain of taking years 'out' of employment often renders part-time study the only route back into higher education. Family and work commitments, the emotional and physical strains of juggling various aspects of lifestyle, and the euphoria at having 'done it' all make part-time academic study a unique and rewarding experience.

However, little material currently exists regarding the issues that affect those who study part-time. There seems to be an inherent assumption that the postgraduate student is a *full-time* student. The social and emotional issues of postgraduate study are largely neglected, with a defined focus on the technicalities of gaining the qualification. (Such as Phillips and Pugh's *How to Get a PhD, a Handbook for Students and their Supervisors* (1994) Open University Press.) It is for this reason that this text came into being; bringing together a cross section of part-time students, all with differing perspectives and experiences.

Some issues, nevertheless, unite the accounts. Each author identifies difficulties with time management. Structuring and maintaining a balance between the academic, employment and social spheres remains a constant challenge, with one aspect usually dominating the others. Effective organisation stems largely from a process of personal trial and error, especially if education is not the individual's highest priority. This is particularly true when the student is a parent. University attendance, research and writing have to be carefully planned and scheduled with nothing left to chance. However, as readers will discover, the end result is a real family achievement, with all involved in some way or another.

Unfortunately, isolation is another issue that many students have to address. Part-time study can be solitary, with long bouts of seclusion and little contact with other students. For those attending university in the evenings, social facilities that full-time students take for granted, such as coffee bars and common rooms, may be unavailable. Each of the authors suggest that new students create a network of colleagues, that meet regularly, as early as possible. Not only do such networks provide valued academic input and comment, they can also offer emotional support and help bring their members through the 'lows'.

It is true to say that part-time study can throw up a host of new challenges that full-time students may never experience. But the satisfaction gained from realising individual potential and goals, in spite of adversity, can never be underestimated.

Thanks

I would like to thank each of the contributors for creating such well crafted pieces. The rapidity of their production was very much appreciated. May they all have the success they deserve.

Thanks also to John Wakeford, Anne Grinyer, Julie Rossall, Sue Weldon and Jon Clark for unlimited advice and support and for saintly levels of patience throughout.

Hurdles to Gaining Employment

Martin Brocklebank

Martin is currently studying part-time towards a Masters degree in Creative Writing. He is actively searching for employment to support his studies.

She came and got me just as we were about to start considering the things that might stop us from getting a job. Mick, one of the louder members of the group, had launched into another rant about the evils of the system when the door opened and she poked her head in. We all looked round and she nodded at me and said: "Action Plan love?"

She took me into the interview room, sat down at her desk and told me to pull up a chair. I banged my knees on the desk front as I sat. She smiled at me. She was about forty, smart suit, big glasses. A badge on her lapel read: Pauline. She began:

"Right Martin love, all we have to do is..."

"Can I," I said, "Can I just ask about Thursday... tomorrow?"

A pause.

"What about tomorrow?" She said.

"It's the day I go and do my MA course... at Lancaster."

A pause. She smiled.

"Well Martin love," she said, "Shall we talk about that when we've finished?"

"...Right", I said.

She picked up a file from the desk and took out my papers. She laid them down on the desk, glanced at each sheet by lifting the top corner with her thumb and forefinger. She smoothed the sheets out and scanned down the top sheet again. I could see the heading: Jobplan Workshop – Action Plan. I'd seen it on Monday, the first day of the workshop. We all had to fill this top sheet in on that first day. Personal Details, Qualifications, Previous Experience.

"Well", she said, "You've been a busy boy getting all these qual's haven't you?"

She smiled at me. I had to smile back. Jesus – a *busy boy*?

"I guess". I raised my eyebrows and nodded a little.

"Hmm...well, all we have to do now is get you an action plan to get you back to work don't we Martin?"

She looked at me and smiled. I guess she wanted me to say something. I nodded again, and muttered "Right". She turned the sheet over and said:

"So, what *are* your employment aims?"

None. No, not true. To be a writer. And get paid for it.

"Lecturing." I said.

She slipped the sheet across to me and held out a pen.

"Well write that down in that box there at the top then Martin," she said.

I took the pen and wrote: 'Lecturing – FE and/or HE'

I looked up, "And writing."

A pause.

"...Scriptwriting?" I said.

A pause.

"There are opportunities.. It pays well..."

"Well write it down there then if you want Martin," she said.

I wrote: 'and Scriptwriting'

"And fill in the next box please love."

Above the next box it said: 'Please summarise why you think this aim is realistic and achievable'

Shit.

"I can write," I said.

"And you have the relevant qualifications and experience?"

"Yeah... I do... and I will have," I said.

"Write it down there then love."

I wrote it down.

This went on for another three sheets. On the last sheet I agreed to: 1) Continue my Jobsearch (including: visit the jobcentre, contact at least two employers per week, check newspapers and visit websites) and 2) Gain full-time employment (in Lecturing or Screenwriting).

"Well that wasn't too bad was it Martin love," she said. "You can go back to the group now..."

"...What about tomorrow?"

A pause.

"Ye know I go to uni on a Thursday... They know downstairs... where I sign... I told them I'd started the course...," I said.

"Yes, but the Jobplan Workshop lasts for a full week love."

"Yeah I know but - "

"And you're required to attend for the full week."

"I know but –"

"Every day."

"Right but - "

"Or you have to do it all again... It's the law."

She smiled at me. I had to smile back.

"Did they not explain that when they told you that you had to come?" She said.

"Well yeah, but I just thought..."

"What?"

"That ye could make an exception," I said.

"...No love," she said. She smiled and shook her head. I looked away from her, then turned back:

"All this is all supposed to help me get a job yeah?"

She nodded.

"Well that's why I'm doing the MA, yeah, to help me get a job... writing... or lecturing... the things I've put down here," I said and pointed to the forms on the desk.

She nodded, slowly.

"...D'ye know what it's cost me? Nearly, three, grand."

"That's a lot of money," she said.

"Yeah... yeah it is, it is. And, and I've taken out a three grand *career, development,* loan to pay for - "

"Do they know about that downstairs?"

"What?"

"About the CDL?"

"...Yeah."

"Because getting that amount of money could effect your benefits."

I shook my head. I looked away again. I had to.

"I'm going tomorrow." I said and turned back to her.

She smiled. Then she picked up the receiver of the telephone on her desk and punched in three numbers. After a moment she began to speak.

"...June? Yeah hiya love it's... yeah... no... no... ye joking... yeah... ye do right love... yeah... no... nooo... (she laughed)... bloody hell... listen June love, I've got a young gentleman here - "

She put her hand over the mouthpiece and looked at me.

"I'll let you know what they say," she snapped. She waited.

I got up and went back to Mick's rant.

"You've got two options," she said. We were stood in the corridor.

She'd come and got me out of the group just as we were about to get on to considering those things that might stop us from getting a job. We'd each been given a sheet of A4 to write these things down on. The sheet was headed: 'Hurdles to Gaining Employment'. Just below this heading there was a cartoon of a runner striding over a hurdle. And then numbered spaces.

"One, you can go and do your course tomorrow... and you'll have to do the whole week's workshop again..."

I shook my head a little, smiled.

"Or two, you can miss going to Lancaster for this once."

I smiled a little wider. I had to.

"That's not really two options is it?" I said.

We stared at each other. I looked away down the corridor. At the end of the corridor were the double doors that opened into the stairs and led down to the door on the street.

"I'm going anyway." I said.

"You'll just get a letter telling you when to come again for another week."

I nodded. A little. I turned back to her.

"Fine." I turned and walked away and went back to the group and the A4 sheet and the guy jumping over the hurdle.

I went to Lancaster on Thursday. I'm waiting for the letter.

Afterword

He didn't get that letter. But he was ready for it to drop through his letterbox. He was going to appeal. This is what he would write:

- He was attending the MA in order to improve his chances of getting a job.
- He had taken out a Career Development Loan in order to do the MA.
- When told he had to go to the Jobplan Workshop, he wasn't offered the option of attending on a week when he did not have to attend university.
- He had already attended the full week of workshops, apart from the day he had gone to his workshop. Moreover, he had been an active member of the group.
- He had not missed an MA session and did not intend to in the future.

He never got the letter. It seems sense can prevail - even at the DSS.

Long Distance Relationships

Avril Horseford

Avril Horseford is a full-time lecturer at a Southern institute.
She combines this with study towards an EdD.

A Logistical Nightmare?

In the autumn of 1996, I became a part-time student at the University of Durham. I live and work in London, so long-distance, part-time study was theoretically difficult and virtually impossible when rational and measured practicalities were taken into account.

Yet this was the course that met my needs most closely. Considerations such as travelling from London to Durham whilst performing effectively in a full time educational position were considered. And also ignored. Part of the appeal lay in the fact that this mode of study was different to all of the others that I had previously embarked upon.

Part-Time Scars

I had studied part-time before through every level of the educational structure and was familiar with the demands. Completing a day's teaching and moving to the lecture theatre for a three-hour evening workshop was torturous at the best of times. After completing my Masters degree, I made a silent vow *never* to study in the same manner again. I'm sure that there are other students, after completing four, three-hour written papers and a thesis, who made themselves similar promises. Those of us who continued to teach at the time of the examinations, and for whom 'study leave' and 'sick leave' became interchangeable, could only contemplate further part-time study after a long passage of time. The physical pain of the experience had to fade to some degree.

As a result of the persistent reminders of the practical difficulties, whenever I felt the urge to study at post-Masters level, I contemplated a short and compact course. I reasoned that this would satisfy my study-lust whilst remind myself of the many reasons of why it was a bad idea to inflict this self-imposed level of stress. Yet, throughout the years that passed when I attempted not to embark on long-term, part-time study, I discovered something about myself as a learner. I actually *enjoyed* the activities associated with learning in an almost intangible sense. I loved to research information and loved to read for a purpose. I even appreciated the anxiety of struggling to meet the deadlines. I also gravitated towards other who appreciated my condition and began to acknowledge that a further course was what I really wanted. My domestic and professional life never afforded me the opportunities to experience the emotions I craved, or to share them with others who felt the same.

The Education of Education

It is ironic (but true) that those of us who work in the educational field receive very few opportunities to reflect on the issues and processes that we experience over the course of a working day. Although many are comfortable discussing their subject, lessons, or the institutional politics, there is generally a reluctance to bring up the theories and the educational product that these theories support. We are constrained by time, inclination and language. On a day to day basis, education can be delivered in a lonely vacuum. By the time that the results of our tuition become evident, we have moved on to the next subject, class or policy. There are, however, those who relish conversation about the theory, and less the mechanics of education. I am one of these people.

This interest in how education 'worked' allowed me to forget my misgivings about combining part-time study with full-time work. Indeed, my career in education would become central to my doctorate so I was keen to find a course that would allow me to use my professional practices as the basis of my research. Not only did this satisfy my employers - who I hoped would partly fund the research - but it also allowed me to use sources of data that were immediately accessible, familiar and consistent. Such sources required little prior arrangement; something that is integral to external sources. I had given these issues careful thought before applying to the Doctorate of Education at the University of Durham.

One of the reasons that I favoured this course was because it was not a doctorate in philosophy - it was a specific and unapologetic doctorate in education. I believed it would address educational issues more readily rather than trying to adhere to the philosophy framework usually required for the completion of a PhD. The course further appealed as it was part taught. Although I had been active in education for many years - there were issues that had bypassed me due to the radical changes that had occurred during my time as a teacher. Specialising and progression often mean that practitioners do not have a full grasp of the issues that affect their student's learning and the delivery of their teaching. I welcomed the opportunity to participate in different methods and 'refresh' upon the concepts I had learned.

The Concrete Course

The course was delivered in three phases. Part one consisted of three compulsory units which set the pace and the agenda of the first year's study. These units also improved our knowledge of key issues and reacquainted us with the practical demands of research - this research would lead to the production of substantial essays at the end of each unit. Phase Two consisted of much of the same, whilst Phase Three required the production of a 40,000 word thesis - something that seems quite unimaginable to the part-time student.

However, long-distance attendance proved to be less of an obstacle than I had originally perceived. The compulsory, taught units required personal presence during the first year, but as the course progressed and became less rigid in its delivery, so too did the pattern of attendance. By the second year, I was required to attend by arrangement only with my supervisors. Very few universities offered this option part-time, and this mode of study ensured that travelling did not dominate my time.

The structure of the course also accommodated part-time, long-distance study. Instead of the usual weekly lectures, instruction was delivered in only two visits per term, each of which lasted from Thursday evening to midday Saturday and offered an intensive programme in a condensed format.

Long-Distance Learning

This model of attendance had many advantages. Firstly, accommodation was provided by the university, which greatly lessened any potential anxiety. Secondly, many of us were involved with demanding work within other institutions. The course allowed for our complete removal from other responsibilities and allowed us to unwind. Nonetheless, several students were often to be found shouting into mobile phones in the corridors and some were summonsed back to work to sort out urgent problems.

As the course progressed, many of us agreed that travelling to participate in our part-time studies was one of the key elements to enjoying it. Often more important than the content of our study, was the support that we received from each other. We were all swamped with similar difficulties at similar times and this strengthened our sense of camaraderie. The educational discussions that we were unable to have at our places of work, we had with each other. And when we lacked momentum, or were simply too exhausted to deliver what was required of us, there was always a barrage of motivational and emotional support.

Teamwork

The course provided a ready-made network of colleagues and research data, coming as we did from schools, further and higher educational institutions, the private sector, home and abroad. Subsequently, when we required detailed information about an area that lay outside our particular specialism, we were able to gather the information from within our group.

Group support is possibly one of the most positive aspects of part-time study and can mean the difference between success and failure. A supportive group can help individuals work through their 'weaker' areas of study because it aids the individual in acknowledging that all students have certain areas that are less strong than others. A group that works well harbours less competition and shares a higher degree of 'favours'. Group members know that each article or reference shared will multiply tenfold when the other members pool their literary research. This was certainly a vital research resource within my own course.

Such elements of competition often witnessed in full-time courses seemed to be absent in our mode of study. We were too engaged in the day to day problems and intricacies of our full-time work to harbour petty jealousies. Also, we did not meet often enough to identify the negative aspects of one another's characters. The two days we together proved long enough to leave Durham without negative memories and also served to provide positive anticipations for our next meetings.

Soon after becoming a student on the EdD, I became part of the course team for a new part-time degree in my own establishment. My own experiences gave me greater insight into the importance of group dynamics in determining the quality of the student experience - and possibly the outcome of study. In mirroring students' experiences, I began to recognise regular, shared patterns, which although not scientific, occurred frequently amongst the people I taught and those with whom I studied.

It became apparent that a large proportion of part-time students decided to embark upon the course that they had been 'putting off' after a long period of time - and the closure of a sometimes traumatic, life-changing event. It seemed that an important personal situation prompted many to conclude, 'it's now or never.' The need to engage upon a new challenge provided a resolution which would establish and begin the individual's return to full strength. On a personal level, I applied for my course as I reached the end of a six-month period of sick leave. My own experience aided my recognition of those who were newly bereaved, newly divorced, and those who were trying to regain their health or overcome a period of personal distress. However, there were also many students whose lives were not nearly so dramatic and had different study motivations.

Exclusion Issues

Another issue we shared as part-time students is that which could be broadly termed 'seniority'. Within the modern educational framework most adult students study part-time, and their needs and responsibilities differ greatly from their more 'junior' peers. Seniority, demonstrated though career, family and financial commitments, often disbars people such as myself from being serious candidates for full-time courses. Unlike younger students, who study free of other commitments, part-time students add the demands of their courses to their existing personal pressures and have to devise specific coping strategies.

Issues of exclusion remain prominent amongst part-timers. On the whole, many fail to become integrated within their university community, with all its benefits and frustrations. I attended many lectures outside of business hours and was sometimes required to use half-closed buildings, which lacked canteen and library facilities - the normal services that full-time students take for granted. Not being taught in an adequate learning environment can easily lead to the feeling that you are a 'second rate' student receiving a second rate product. The fact is, that part-time study can bear few of the hallmarks associated with 'traditional' and 'established' education. Much of the part-time challenge lies within recognising these factors and adapting accordingly.

In brief

- Combining full-time work and part-time study can be gruelling. Selecting courses carefully is intrinsic to completion.

- Studying long distance affords the opportunity for the student to remove themself entirely from work commitments.

- Creating a close social network with peers can be exceptionally beneficial.

A Family Affair

Dawne Gurbutt
A mother and academic, Dawne is studying part-time for a PhD.
Her husband is also studying at another University.

At the moment, my whole family is doing a PhD - or at least that is what it feels like. In reality, the two adults are doing a PhD, but such is the nature of our study, that the effects are widespread. Conversation often turns to research and supervision, so much so that our children have taken this on board. Chatter with small friends from infant school can quickly turn to the timetables of our research, such as "Well, we're going there - when Mummy and Daddy have finished their research". This interest has infected our household to epidemic proportions. So, how did we arrive at this situation?

The Roots

My husband and I both worked as academics at a local university and had also studied for Masters degrees. Although we worked at separate times, our interests were mutual as we both covered similar subjects. Gearing up for 'the big one' followed when my husband won a bursary to register for a PhD. We pontificated at length about the amount of time this would consume, and more importantly, the effect it would have on our family life. But owing to his enviable ability to work at length in the small hours and the opportunity to take a research job which would enable him to maximise his study time, we rose to the situation and slotted the work into out daily lives.

He often spoke about the research and fieldwork he was embarking upon, and although it was obviously challenging - it proved a manageable, and seemingly productive, use of time. It also had an added bonus; it was mentally stimulating. I began to concede that at some point in the future, with my husband's PhD safely behind us and firmly in 'rose tinted' territory, that I too would move into the same type of study. However, even the best laid plans of mice, men and female academics are prone to going astray. Subsequently, I found myself casually surfing the Internet at work. And yes, I 'stumbled' upon the ideal studentship for a PhD. I wanted to apply.

Household Review Number Two: if I were successful, what would this mean in practice? Could we manage both financially and physically? Did we want to 'spin so many plates' all at once, or was it a somewhat foolhardy suggestion? We already shared the childcare of our two young, school-age children, without external childcare arrangements. Synchronising of diaries, great amounts of communication and forward planning were already a necessity. But nonetheless - we went ahead and soon discovered that our time management skills were so advanced that even my part time movement to another university wasn't overly problematic.

Family Finances

So what about the financial aspect? Well, a fees-paid bursary and a minimal sponsorship meant that in real terms there should have been no additional costs. However this did not take into account lost earnings. There was also the fact that your career is put on hold - you are not free to advance your job prospects in the way you would usually envisage. Many deliberations later, and with all other available strands of income accounted for, (such as ad hoc work and occasional work) we are both registered on PhD programmes. We are both working (some more extensively than others) and both maintain a strong continuation of our 'normal' family life.

And I certainly wouldn't recommend it to the faint-hearted. But for people like us, who share most things in life and enjoy being (and indeed working) together, it has so far proved to be a mutually enjoyable experience - although exhaustion is a definite downside. Nonetheless, the spin offs have been good. Our children are immersed in literature and view discussing their reading as the normal way to behave. They spend time writing and talking about what they have written and seem genuinely pleased that their parents get their names in print from time to time.

Practicalities

But what are the practical points of joint study like this and what does it mean in terms of the 'real world'?   When I first embarked upon my current research, a colleague explained to me that a PhD was all about writing and defending your thesis. At the time, I thought of that in terms of the final viva examination. I have since come to realise that as a mother, a female, an academic, a friend and a member of society - you learn from the outset to 'defend' your work in all sorts of scenarios and at all sorts of times. It becomes a way of life. My research has also become a way of life and an additional member of the family.   I care for it. I nurture it. I devote time to making sure it doesn't feel neglected. (And that I don't guiltily feel I'm neglecting it.) And just like having a new baby, I occasionally show it to close friends and family hoping for admiration and approval. However, although I may wish for the favour of others, it is not always the response which is generated.

Thankfully, there are a couple of notable exceptions. The first of these exceptions is my husband. Tremendous benefit has been gleaned on both sides from studying at different locations but within the same time frame. We are, in a sense, each other's best critics and regularly prepare one another for our respective supervision groups. It's great to have someone who will give you an honest appraisal of your work and find holes in your argument. It's also helpful to have someone who will help you to plug them. We have found that supervision differs greatly between establishments, as do the expectations of the students. By fully discussing our respective supervision sessions, we benefit from having a wider slant and view of opinions on areas such as methodology and philosophical issues. Perhaps this turns us into sad 'anoraks'. Many people would look askance (and do!) at the very sight of the married couple at the next table discussing paradigms.... But each to their own and it works for us.

Access to two university libraries has also been a huge bonus, and that has been an eye opener in itself. Emphasis within establishments on certain approaches and ideas can differ greatly. Studying on two different sites has increased our exposure to peers who are also doing PhD studies. This type of networking - if only to find that we are all part of a wider circle of unconfident writers who feel their conclusions are obvious to everyone - is invaluable. It throws your self-evaluation of progress into the wider context. Interestingly, we have fallen into our own reading group, digesting and then discussing similar articles and chapters. The plus point has been that we have found ourselves supporting other academics (studying long distance from their own institutions) who enjoy a bit of scholarly debate.

An interesting aside to mutual study is that there are times when things are going particularly well. One of us has a spring in their step and this can be quite infectious - ideas seem to flow. At other times, the researcher can have all the enthusiasm of a damp dog and it's good to have a 'coach' on your team who can remind you of better times and encourage you that a 'sunny day' (in research terms) - may be just around the corner.

However envy can brew. When both of us have papers that are due at the same time, it's easy to believe that he can think more quickly than I can, but that I'm the faster typist. Although joint projects can reap the benefit of such mixed skills, individual ones lead to a certain amount of controlled but wistful jealously.

Attitudes

Approval? There have been many areas where support is not quite so forthcoming. Work colleagues can be less than supportive of another's PhD study. There is a sense that those doing research may be treated more favourably by their institutions (totally unfounded in most cases I have come across). My inquiries regarding the progress of others' research is frequently met with bristly suspicion, as though I am implying some deep-rooted criticism of their work. For others, a PhD seems to be viewed as a subversive activity which can only be discussed in whispers, and has no place in the usual 'cut and thrust' of academic conversation.

The photocopy room has been a low-key hive of support where colleagues can often be caught copying material of great scholarly interest. Similar academic interests can lead to further rendezvous that are highly enjoyable and academically beneficial. I was recently stopped by a member of staff whilst walking between meetings. He had heard about my research through the 'copier room' grapevine and had taken the trouble to print a couple of his own articles for my perusal - a scholarly and generous gesture which restored my faith in my wider group of colleagues.

Part-Time Work

If you work part time, your PhD study is widely ignored by employers. It falls into the 'useful hobby' category, and although it may blossom into a gracious appendage to your CV and act as a plinth to your career, there is an almost unspoken rule that nobody wants to acknowledge its existence in the meantime. Colleagues mutter darkly about the number of academics who start PhDs but never finish them, and you always feel that they would love to add you to their gloomy statistics... Although it would be nothing to do with them, of course.

The PhD and the School Yard

Some view the PhD students with a level of respect as massive academic thinkers (totally undeserved I must add.) Others congratulate you on your achievement and organisational skills, but this is usually intertwined with comments about how much they value motherhood. The richest vein of contradictory feeling is experienced at my children's school. I never willingly reveal what I do with my time, but mothers have a knack of finding out. Many feel that I am 'only a student' and therefore low in the Parent Pecking Order. 'PhD' may increase my student status, but not by much. Views vary - a waste of time and of taxpayers' money; an example of self indulgence as a mother all contrasted with those who have no idea of what I am talking about.

Interestingly, I have another persona inside the school. I'm a 'classroom' or 'parent helper'. This provides a lovely occasional break from the rigours of academic thinking, and is a constant reminder of how much we have all had to learn at one time of another. The parent helper is perceived by staff as being a non-academic, and therefore the simplest tasks, such as switching on a photocopier or using a guillotine, are explained in minute detail. This is the great leveller.

However much I have been grappling with philosophical issues; however much I feel that I have much more to offer in terms of scholarly debate; however much I may feel, (at times) that I am beginning (at last) to think and act like a scholar - when I go into school I am just me. A mum. And I can receive detailed advice on how to successfully fill a glue pot. Am I likely to become arrogant or self inflated? I think not. Some things PhD study will change for ever, but some will always remain the same.

Which brings me back neatly to where I began. It is a family affair, this studying for a PhD. Away from my supervision team and fellow students, it is only my family which sees the graft and the effort. They notice the minute changes and listen to the questions you ask of yourself and of others. It is the family who make allowances for your work, make sure that your writing is kept safe, relocate lost books, and occasionally make do with a fast food meal. My children feel good about Mummy and Daddy studying. A sense of justice prevails - we all do 'homework' and 'reading for school'. We all realise its importance. That is why, when (and indeed, if,) we both graduate, it will be our family that has made the grade.... The celebration will include us all ...A real family affair.

Afterword

- When both parents are involved in part-time study, communication is integral to organisation.

- Children can benefit a great deal from parents' study. Learning and literacy is viewed as natural and desirable.

- Actively seek support and comment from those around you. Colleagues and partners can provide a ready-made network.

A Path Less Travelled

Russell Gurbutt

Russell currently works as a lecturer and is studying for a PhD.
He is married to Dawne and is a father.

This reflection includes considerations about why I bothered to study for a higher research degree and the relationships that were affected as a result; be they between myself, family, colleagues, supervision staff or other researchers. Part-time study can feel like a path less travelled - the occasional company of companions interspersed with long bouts of solitude

Why a Higher Degree?

Laurie Lee wrote in 'Cider with Rosie' that he was born at the end of a thousand years of rural history. Living at the turn of the millennium makes me feel that I exist just after the golden age of employment. Indeed, to establish some job-security seems to require a versatility of being able to craft a CV towards emerging employment opportunities. In the field of higher education this seems to require the academic to accumulate a range of 'experiences' on their CV. These might be publishing, winning research funding bids and speaking at conferences. To achieve this requires a series of decisions - the first of which for me was to set the priority order of attaining these goals. My first priority was to gain a higher degree by research. I had decided that this would be a relevant and useful career development step in Health Studies and sought for a working solution to facilitate the start of that journey.

There were also other interests at work. I saw a benefit in building on the professional development gained through my first two degree courses. Furthermore, I felt that it might be good to spend a prolonged period of my life enjoying the mental stimulation of academic study.

Options

To achieve this I was faced with two options: one was to fund the study myself and the second was to draw funding from elsewhere. There was also the issue of where I would study. In the final analysis the latter was resource driven. My current university was cheaper and local, whereas a competitor establishment thirty miles away was both more expensive but better rated in RAE terms. I was subsequently to discover that the quality of research supervision arrangements might actually be reflected in both the costs and the ratings.

Winning funding for five years was the first success towards my studies and this was further maximised by gaining an alumni discount on fees. In all, the bursary does seem to create an added interest by the institution in the student. I suppose, in blunt terms, they are eager to see that the award contributes towards producing a successful outcome. I therefore commenced upon a five year part time M. Phil / PhD

Sidelines

During the first year I took up a post as a research assistant which was a valuable adjunct to learning about the practical issues of research design. I then secured a lecturing post in a health department at the sponsoring institution. For the term of the lectureship contract, financial concerns were given some stability. The limited tenure of the contract led to a decision to try and complete the part time study within its original span.

Family Relationships.

A speaker at the university induction day claimed that the study would be like a marriage. I felt at the time that this was a bit of hype. In fact, I don't view it as a marriage but more like a friendship. However, the time factor involved could be what the speaker was alluding to. Higher degree students are recommended to undertake a minimum of twelve hours study per week - but that is akin to specifying the length of a piece of string. In the course of other work I find myself thinking about issues in relation to the research and by default develop evaluative and critical skills.

Time pressures can affect family life if the art of juggling the different demands is not developed. These included the care and ferrying around of our two children to and from school and extra curricular activities. Sharing roles and flexible patterns of work have enabled us to achieve this. Some time is sacrosanct, such as Saturdays and meals out with the whole family. Weekends away also provide a change of scenery and a break from the temptation to work

<u>Colleagues</u>

The university in theory has a mission of teaching and research activity, however at times it can appear to be what a friend called a 'teaching factory'. Research, and remission for research time, seems to be viewed by some as the ultimate in lead swinging. It has been my experience that those without a higher degree have always got a reason to devalue it or to say why it is not necessary for them to study for one. That's life, I suppose, but is not a reason to be diverted from personal goals.

The increasing workload demanded in H.E. often means that there is a role overload. It is essential, therefore, to know what you can do within the time available and to be able to quantify what you are already doing. Otherwise there is a danger of the research time being eroded. I found that giving too much leeway to university commitments only erodes the time for the research and ultimately it is never clawed back.

The Experience of Supervision

My research study has been supervised by a team of three staff. This experience, however, seems to be as individual as the interpersonal dynamics of the team. Whilst there are some useful text-sharing insights into the supervision experience and they were useful in contemplating the way ahead, it is necessary to 'give it a go' before any hard and fast judgements are made. Two key issues have arisen out of my supervision experience: the ownership of the research and the management of the relationship with the supervisors.

Ownership and Management

Whilst supervision is designed to support the student, it can on occasions appear to be the image of formal support operated by the university whilst lacking a sense of personal investment in the individual. In terms of ownership, the study remains mine to be presented in various forms at different times to satisfy stages of the university process. The administrative system creates periodic bursts of focused activity as you progress through designated stages of the research plan. This process can seek to shape the research and thus can try to alter the focus - hence the need to retain ownership. Nevertheless, the dust settles and you can then get back to interesting aspects of the work.

The management of the team relationship has been a developmental experience. In the initial stages I was quite passive in accepting who was recommended to be a part of the team. But as time progressed, I became convinced of the need to own the study and to be more assertive in making my requirements explicit. During my first year, one of the second supervisors left closely followed by the director of studies. This required negotiation with the third member of the team to pull together what was effectively a new team to keep the supervision arrangements on track. Whilst it caused a little angst at the time, the cloud had a silver lining. My former director of studies never gave full individual attention to me during set meetings. The room was always being interrupted or shared with another lecturer and the director was frequently doing some other activity whilst giving part attention to my conversation. So a change to someone who would actually listen and give considered advice was welcomed. One further issue was that the recommended choice of words to include in the registration document by the then director, became problematic at a later stage. With hindsight I should have been more questioning of their particular methodological perspective and clearer about the other options open to find the data that would address my research question. It sounds simple, but at the time there were so many things to consider that what later emerges as quite a central issue, is absorbed in the general backdrop of other issues. I think part of higher degree work is to learn about the nature of the process.

Supervisor Relationships

The relationship with the supervisors is both friendly and political. Let's get real here. The student is paying for the supervision through their fees. The supervisors want to augment their portfolio of successful supervisees. And the university wants to ensure that completion is achieved. The high percentage of people who do not submit a thesis on a PhD program can make you feel like a crewman on a wartime bomber. The attrition rate seems to be so great that does it become inevitable? Well, I think not, but it is useful to try and find out why other students never complete. Actual hard data about this seems to be difficult to come by and the essence of it is held in snatches of conversations and second hand reports. To recognise that there must be some huge threat to successful completion, I have decided to proceed on what I know: the requirement of the academic processes and maintaining my focus to keep to a strict time schedule. At this stage, this equation is my best strategy towards completion.

Networking and other Students

Universities ideally have a research culture, but if that is still in a developmental phase then it is necessary to press on and develop your own networks to serve the purposes of research and academic development. The university provides several supportive opportunities to find out about other staff and student research studies. Beyond that, there are informal students' groups. However, working pressures have meant that I have rarely used these arrangements. My most beneficial networks have been constructed through attending conferences and joining electronic networks. A self-help strategy has been the preferred option probably because no one can sit you down and point you to specific help, only offer general guidance. Using the internet and subscribing to several mail bases which allow for live discussions on related topics [www.mailbase.ac.uk] have proved to be an invaluable resource.

The internet is also a costly and time consuming resource. I find it useful to be doing some other study activity whilst surfing for information as a lot of time can be wasted waiting for a page to load. Computer crashes and viruses have also led me not to rely solely on electronic media to store the data and text of the research.

Partners in Research

The best network has been my wife, who decided that she could do a PhD too and promptly registered at a five star institution. This has allowed me to tap into other electronic networks, find out first hand about a different experience of supervision and look at the working arrangements for supporting research activity. That has been as useful as my own supervision in preparing for the submission and viva voce examination. This arrangement has worked well for us but would have failed if we were not supportive of one another.

<u>Conclusion</u>

I commenced this reflection by saying that it felt like a path less travelled and making reference to the people affected by the research. This path requires many decisions to take regarding time, funding and maintaining a life beyond work and research. However I have changed through the experience and my family has altered through the shared experience of this journey. Perhaps it is now becoming part of us and our lifestyle. It is the strength of that which now contributes to achieving our goals in working as lecturers in H.E., in a workload and time pressured environment. Thus with the goal in sight and the realisation that we are all seeing life differently having travelled some distance over the past two years, it is worth pressing on.

In Brief

- Course costs can often be reflected in the standards of teaching and facilities.

- Maintaining strength of focus is essential throughout.

- Discussion and support networks are invaluable. Check the Net for relevant groups.

The Part Time MA Business

Rosie Stevens
Rosie studied for an MA in Management Learning. She combined much of this study with a demanding development role within a public sector organisation.

The Big Questions

I sat in Anna Lorbiecki's room wondering, not for the first time, what on earth I thought I was doing there. Anna is a Teaching Director and Director for the MA in Management Learning and I had come for my interview – or, more honestly, to assess my suitability to undertake such a demanding part time course of study.

There was no doubt that I had completely taken leave of my senses. Here I was, purporting to be able to take on a huge extra workload, when I was already overwhelmed by the sheer size of the project I had just taken on at work. I liked my job, but it was becoming increasingly demanding, both mentally and physically. I worked in a relatively senior organisational development role in a large public sector company. I not only travelled two hours each way to my normal base, but also covered the whole of London and the South East, which meant frequent nights away from home and days where my car journey could be anything between six and eight hours (depending, of course, on the M25).

I was permanently exhausted and often wondered how I was going to drag myself through the day. Like everyone else, I usually overcame this lethargy by about 10 o'clock in the morning, visibly livening up, becoming positively energetic by lunchtime and managing to retain this energy through until late evening. But sleep was often fitful and interrupted by the long list of things I had to remember and do that week, and the next morning began with the same overwhelming exhaustion and longing for more holiday.

So what, then, was I doing, sitting in this institution of eminent academia, earnestly – and hopefully convincingly – talking about my great enthusiasm for the MA in Management Learning, or MAML as it is better known? And who did I think I was, when Anna challenged my academic ability to do a higher degree, (given that I did not have a first degree) assuring her that I was undoubtedly intellectually capable? I even gave her examples to back it up. (A trick I had learned from my extensive involvement in competency based recruitment, promotion and appraisal.)

And why, exactly, was I doing it? Did I not have enough pressures squeezed into my life? Did I not already feel guilt about being unable to do everything I should, both at work and at home? What impact would this extra burden have on my already long-suffering partner and daughter? And, more to the point, could I *really* do it?

If the truth be told, I was scared – both of rejection (from course entry) and failure (if I started and wasn't up to scratch.) But something inexplicable drove me on. Call it my age – 45 – call it pride; call it stupidity; but I felt I had reached a time in my life when there was something missing. I'm not sure that I knew what it was then, but have since concluded that it was the need to learn. The need to be really challenged - to feel that I had moved on in terms of greater understanding, (of what I wasn't sure) yet I felt instinctively that there *was* more to understand than the mere complexities of a new job.

The Bigger Realities

Remarkably, I was accepted. I was excited, nervous, afraid, eager, delighted and very daunted. I turned up at the first workshop with a feeling of great trepidation. Who else would be on the course? What would they be like? Would they all be supremely intellectual? Would they think I was stupid?

MAML workshops are held at a magnificent, rambling old house. The staff are delightful and extremely helpful, the food is marvellous – but very fattening – and the views quite spectacular. The surroundings are instantly soothing and, more importantly, away from the hustle and bustle of city working life. Time seemed unimportant and work faded to a distant memory...

Each workshop has a different theme and gives people the opportunity to explore, as and how they wish, the complexities of management learning. The first workshop was initially tutor-led but moved swiftly to being participant directed. The whole ethos of MAML is that of building a learning community, who will work together and support each other throughout the whole programme. I even hesitate to call it a programme, as very little is actually programmed but is developed by the community as members work and learn together. This support became essential throughout the course.

This was not an entirely new concept, grounded as I was in Human Resources, and yet it felt entirely different to anything I had ever experienced. By the end of day one, twenty-one people were chatting animatedly, comparing stories and experiences and actually having fun. The atmosphere was euphoric. I could not have been luckier in the bunch of people who were to be my fellow learners. There was no one with a huge ego. There was no one person who was singularly difficult or obnoxious. Everyone liked each other. Training and development specialists would normally say that, within any group of people, there is always 'one'. But there wasn't.

Together, we drew up a set of agreed values which represented important principles about the way we wanted to work for the two year duration of the MA. We reviewed daily how things were going and how we felt. We played riotous games in the bar every night. We drank lots of very reasonably priced booze - and here I have to say that I suspect the southerners amongst us made the most of such refreshingly cheap alcohol.

And so it was that we entered our first week, in a spirit of comradeship, fun and adventure. It all seemed so easy… until it dawned on us that we actually had some serious academic work to do, and moreover, that we had to do our first seminar paper quite quickly. Oh dear! This was getting a bit too much like hard work. We began to get fidgety and worried.

Assessment Nightmares

Even more daunting was the discovery that we had to form learning sets and mark each other's work. The tutors were, in theory, to be equal members of the learning set, working with the principal that everyone has their own set of experiences, their own wealth of largely untapped professional knowledge and their own particular gifts and potential.

How on earth could that possibly work? We knew nothing of academic rigour and standards. Even those amongst us with first degrees in related subjects had no idea how to mark an MA paper. We were also acutely aware that the University had a five-star rating, not least for its work in the management learning field and therefore had its considerable reputation to uphold. This was seemingly bizarre. It could never work. And yet we were reassured by the team that they had run sixteen previous MAMLs and that indeed it could and did work, standing up perfectly well to an extremely stringent external verification process.

My first paper was one I would probably rather forget; not because I failed it – in fact, I did fairly well – but because I have to confess that I hadn't a clue what I was doing for most of the six or seven weeks I had to write it in. This was a nasty shock compared to the cosiness of the first workshop. I felt alternately as though I had at long last been inspired and then let down to discover that I had seemingly missed the point again. I often felt utterly stupid, muddled, dismayed and stressed. I had a mountain of work to do for my day job and very little time to read or even understand the difficult academic critical theory to which we were being introduced. I often read and re-read paragraphs of text in a futile attempt to understand not only their complex arguments but even their vocabulary.

I, and my partners-in-crime, giggled over our apparent inability to get to grips with this whole new language. I bought *The Oxford Dictionary of Sociology*, to look up words such as 'pedagogy', 'subjectivism', 'humanistic', 'phenomenological paradigms' - and 'ontological perspective', which I discovered was nothing to do with eyes or birds but was, in its simplest form, a scale of beliefs about the way the world is. This that this explanation is overly simplistic, lacking depth of understanding and will be tutted over by many in the academic community.

Eventually, it seemed that I managed to understand some of the literature. I still continued to fret over the appropriate use of quotes and referencing and shared a concern with the others about nailing my colours to the mast and attempting my own explanations of complex critical theory. Our first set assessment came and went, and, although none of us felt competent to assess papers at MA standard, or to suggest other referencing which could have been included, we did, it seemed, make a reasonable stab at feedback and marking. The tutor, of course, has to play the role of adjudicator, ensuring that the marks awarded by the set reflect MA standards and will stand up to external verification. Although, strangely, it is rare that there is a great gulf between the tutor's marks and those of other set members.

The Academic Paradox

Here, then, was another can of worms waiting to be opened. Once I began to read the critical theory written by the eminently respected in the academic world, I could no longer remain blissfully ignorant of its existence, nor, indeed, deliberately ignore it – even if I wanted to. And there's the rub. There are several groups of people, it seems, vying for position, posing competing theories, denying them altogether, as in the case of most of us who had been management practitioners. There are management practitioners, management developers, management educators, educationalists, critical theorists and critically reflective practitioners, to name but a few.

So the game, it seems, depends on where you sit. Management practitioners tend to be largely unaware of any of the academic critical theory, given that it is largely written by academics, for the academic community. Managers are therefore rarely exposed to it and probably wouldn't understand half of it even if they were and so tend to favour the gurus or management consultants of the day.

Critical theorists (in the truly academic sense) write worthy tomes analysing and, not surprisingly from their own description of themselves, criticising modern organisations for their hierarchies, implicit power bases and dubious manipulative patriarchal practices. Values and mission statements, according to the critical theorists, can merely be a more pleasant way of continuing to manipulate the workforce to do what the senior leadership team wanted it to do anyway, thereby conveniently reinforcing their own power base.

The critically reflective practitioners, however, are aware of – indeed, write much of – the critically reflective literature, but try personally to incorporate that awareness into their own practice and into their external work. This helps to bring management practice and critical reflection closer together.

It is felt by many that critical theory on its own can be destructive, carping as it does from the safety of the sidelines while never getting mud on its clean boots. It does not help managers or organisations to move forward, as it does not generate alternative solutions. It made me feel despondent – even stupid – to have been so seduced by the modern niceties of organisational values, when, according to the critical theorists, their benefits were likely to be superficial and those who believed in them were merely being naive.

I went into indignant denial. How could any of this possibly be right? I had always tried to do my best to make a difference, particularly to the way we worked together in the organisation towards what I believed were common goals. What did they know? Some of them had never set foot in another organisation – at least, not to do an honest day's work.

And yet – I couldn't deny that a lot of it made sense, particularly when I understood better the historical development of organisations and even societies and races. But I was still left with an overwhelming feeling of utter frustration. Assuming that these theories had some foundation, what then should be done about it?

I decided that I could never be a pure critical theorist. (In any case, I am not clever enough!). I know that I am not someone who can give up trying and I need to have something to believe in. So I have concluded that I should make good use of this new awareness which should help to prevent me blundering about like some naive angel of mercy. I have decided to call myself a 'critically reflective practitioner' – partly because it is a longer and more fanciful title and partly because it more accurately reflects what I want to be.

And the Outcome?

My journey into academia started with fun and companionship, but with a complete lack of understanding of what I had let myself in for. It took me through three nail biting papers, all of which I have managed to pass. It brought me from a complete state of bemusement about the complexity of the subject matter and degree of difficulty, at the end of the first workshop, through to a stage of rapid metamorphosis. By the second workshop, I actually understood and was able to participate in discussions where 'big words' were an essential accessory. (I do have to admit to reaching my threshold at around nine o'clock and sloping off to the bar with some other degenerates to partake of more ambient and basic activities, such as drinking, telling jokes and playing stupid games.)

I have come through my continuous self doubt and nerve wracked attempts at academic writing and have learned much to be proud of. I can do it, I have done it and, despite the closest shaves in meeting deadlines, (I work better at the last minute, I keep telling myself) I have managed to complete and submit one or two reasonable attempts at academic writing. I even became brave enough to take the huge gamble of writing my last paper in the form of a 'docu-play' – so called because I wasn't quite clever enough to pull it off as a pure play, as there was too much documentary commentary in it.

I have also left my full time job – not in a fit of pique or critically reflective analysis – in fact, far from it - but because I have given a great deal of thought to the balance of priorities in my life. I have, as the politicians say, left to spend more time with my family.

So would I do it again, I hear you ask? Amazingly, yes I would. I have learned more than I thought possible, or rather, than I knew existed. I have met the most agreeable and likeable group of people, and I have had a lot of fun – a rare commodity in modern life. I have even been asked to write this chapter – the greatest surprise of all. It may never make it into print – indeed, I would be astounded if it did. But I have enjoyed doing it and – as usual – have managed to complete it by the deadline, at the last minute.

In Short

- The need for self-challenge can be the part-timer's main driving force, even during a 'low'.

- Coming to terms with academic discourse can be tiring and demoralising, but perseverance is the only solution.

- Studying your area of employment can dismantle many of the values you previously held. This can be disturbing.

Poems

Martyn Halsall

Martyn is a self confessed 'mature' student working towards an MA in Creative Writing. He currently works for the Church of England.

The evening after my father's funeral, I went down to the beach at Southport, at low water, and walked out to the tide line. A wreck is easily visible at such times, out beyond the pier, as a reminder of the many ships that have foundered on the Lancashire coast. For some time, I had been thinking of writing a sequence of poems about the Mexico disaster - when in 1886, 27 men died trying to rescue the crew of a German barque in Britain's worst lifeboat incident. My father had introduced me to the story when I was a child. We discovered a postcard, sold in aid of the bereaved families, in a trunk in my grandmother's apple loft. Over the next few months I crafted the poetry.

Part of the reason was to codify memories; part of it was to satisfy an audience and part of it was an intellectual demand to produce new work. Some four months after the funeral, I began a part-time MA in Creative writing at an established university. I had applied, and been awarded a place on the course some two or three years earlier when I was still a correspondent for a national newspaper. Whilst *The Guardian* had agreed that I could take a morning off each week to attend university, I could not see how in depth discussion of literary influences could necessarily co-exist with the 'But we need you in Newcastle' demands of a newspaper's ever-frenetic news-desk. So the course waited, in a way, for my own history to arrive a more suitable starting point. Full time study was not an option. My course began just twelve months after I had started a new job. We had a daughter at university and another hoping to qualify. Economics dictated part-time study. Financial pressure was lessened by my new employer, any help with funding is worth pursuing.

The course does not include set texts or examinations; a bonus to those of us with different academic qualifications. To gain this degree you have to create a body of written work and assess some of your fellow students' own material. To extract the maximum benefit, you need to contribute frequently to the weekly sessions, which last, for part-time students, a couple of years. The degree, a pass or distinction, is awarded by the tutors and an examiner who is a critically acclaimed author.

One of the benefits of being a part-time student is working with two contrasting groups of writers, covering various decades and continents. Students sharing my course have come from Canada, Malaysia and the USA. They mixed with people from contrasting regional backgrounds from various areas within the UK. As a considerably mature student in my early fifties, with thirty years in journalism behind me, the course has also introduced me to fresh agendas and literary reference points. Several of the younger writers in my first year had a strongly defined commitment to 'sex'n'drugs'n'rock'n'roll' literature. They rode fairly lightly over the rock'n'roll.

Working over two years also meant a different cocktail of ages and personalities; of writing interests and abilities. An open-ended postgraduate course like this is naturally an amalgam of what is taught and what is brought; the results succeeding as individuals add their own perspectives and translations. Being an older member of a primarily younger group can be both inclusive and isolating. I live an hour's drive away from my university and am thus unlikely to meet other students outside of classes. This gives the course an imbalance. There is no social life. It means that you meet other students only at workshops and do not know them very well. You learn primarily about the writing lives of otherwise quite mysterious people. You play a guessing game about where their writing is disclosing their lives and personalities. You also miss out on the informal activities, the discussion, drinks and readings, which inform and stimulate the lives of creative writers and add an essential social dimension to the solitary hours with the scrap paper and the keyboard.

This underlines two necessities for detached part-time study on this type of course; that you want to write and that you have to believe in what you are writing. That is not to deny the need for constant reassessment and revision. But I have felt it important to try to develop a body of work that has both critical validity and artistic assurance. The longer the course has continued, the more elusive both of these ideals have appeared.

During the 'middle' summer, I received several emails form potential students. "What was the course like?" they wanted to know. Should they accept places offered? The guidance I tried to provide was this: that to benefit from the course you need to want to write, and to write a lot. For the part-time student, this means juggling writing with other commitments. People ask, "When do you write?" The answer is usually when there is a free moment. Creativity needs to be rapidly summoned and revised.

My background has helped. Journalism is intolerant of time, demands rapid assembly and assessment of information, and is eager for a clear direction through a piece of writing. It is severe on waffle and flannel. A journalist has to also be prepared for others to exercise their writing and editing input on the final text. There are parallels with creative writing, when assessed through workshops. I have been a grateful member of the course for a couple of years, which has given time for a longer period of self-critical assessment and revision, and the development of new themes. I would have found the pressure greater in preparing an equivalent body of work over a shorter period of time, facing two workshops a week, even though there was theoretically more 'ree' time within which to work. I know that being on the course has made me write work which would have otherwise crumbled on the rear shelves of the brain, as potential ideas never realised. The fact that some of the work has already been published adds currency to the creative urgency.

There is obviously no guarantee that my material will ever appear in print. At least two schools of thought appear to assemble around creative writing courses. One underlines the 'creative' as part of encouraging life towards comprehensive personal fulfilment. The other emphasises the 'writing' as a personal craft, the goal of which is public appearance and appreciation. I would like at least some of the work I am producing to be published, and hope that the chances of publication will be enhanced by what I have learned as a student. The degree itself, at my age, is quite likely to be literally academic. Any editor's acceptance slip is far stronger motivation that a cap and gown. No poet is going to be able to brandish a post-graduate qualification as a passport to the career move escalator.

Criticism is not to be considered an exercise at the expense of others, or the wilful distribution of negativity. Constant and essential criticism works in both directions as you contribute to the development of other people's work, and as they comment on what you have written. The full-time students have two such sessions a week and write for two different tutors; one specialising in fiction and the other in poetry. The part-time students' weekly sessions offer no concessions about the standard of work required. Each student has responsibility for their own professional standards.

Where the part-time student may be at a disadvantage is in potential day to day contact with academic support staff, although individual meetings are arranged for each student, with a tutor, once a term. It must also be easier for full-time students to maintain a 'thread' or 'flow' in their work, particularly for those engaged on a novel. They are able to weave its progress between two tutors with different approaches every few days. I believe the quality of work submitted cannot be divided between full and part time students, though full time students are noticeably swifter in resubmitting work after revision.

The poet, Peter Scupham, has been among those likening the writing of poetry to dipping a bucket in a well. There is a body of experience on which you begin to draw. A poem is produced, but then there is an associated idea, or another chapter of memory or a tangential image, as if the bucket were being lowered again. I have found that enforced, regular writing has made me more diligent with the bucket. Instead of random work, there has been more of a direction; essential if you are looking towards publishing a collection with its own narrative force; its unique history and drive. The part-time nature of study accentuates this, giving both an impetus for the creation of new work allowing space between weekly visits to revise work in the context of the domestic and the everyday. Such experience - and the extra steams of memory and contributed reading - are sieved and evaluated.

There can be a positive balance in the course, particularly helpful to part-time students needing to be both creative, and to write. Some, particularly younger students who would enjoy the informal solidarity which university life supplies, might find it easier to create in a settled environment. I find the experiences of the days between university visits often supply the ideas for the development of new work.

The absence of a set recommended reading list does not preclude a considerable recommended reading. This includes both contemporary literature and those working in the areas of creativity and literary technique. Any part-time student should receive encouragement to develop their work by being a member of the university, with access to libraries, lectures, (if these can be fitted in) and the conception of other students' encouragement and analysis. But always, in the background, is the pressure of time. There are those weeks when the workshop looms without any words having been placed on paper. Such pressure can form part of the creative process. Perhaps, it has to be that simple application of pen to paper which kick-starts the creativity. A line might be drafted in near-desperation, but as work continues another idea begins to form and at least some form of creative work has started.

Time may not always be so flexible to employers. I have been fortunate to be employed by a *Church of England* diocese which recognises that value of study and has provided encouragement through the guarantee of appropriate time to attend the university for weekly sessions. The diocese has also provided a generous degree of financial support. It is difficult to imagine part-time study being possible in my former job as a newspaper journalist, where the immediate always over-rides longer term commitments.

In one sense, although I was always nervous about arriving before the bell, I had always been late for school. I began grammar school at the age of twelve, having failed the 11+ and only went to prep school at eighteen, as a student teacher. To that extent, I have always been a late developer. If you had suggested to the gowned master who taught me in the bottom stream of a seaside grammar that I would one day study for a master's degree, they would have replied with a patronising smile. I was not necessarily expected to achieve sufficient GCE results to return to the sixth form. A careers master advised my parents that I might be employed in a book shop as I 'seemed to like reading'.

This is perhaps the greatest stimulus for studying part-time for a higher degree, to enjoy what had previously been denied. To many people, it awards eventual recognition that you are capable of fulfilling stringent academic demands; that the dream was not futile but a rehearsal of potential.

Reflections

- The time between university visits can be utilised to provide fuel for the imagination.

- Maturity can be an isolating factor for part-time student.

- Part-time study can provide the opportunity to enjoy an education that has been previously denied and stretch individual boundaries.

A Part Time Philosophy

Rachel Jones

Rachel began as a full-time Social Sciences PhD student, but switched to part-time to finance her studies.

I initially started my PhD as a full-time research student at a new university. It was an inter-disciplinary research project that was broadly based within the social sciences. However, various difficulties emerged towards the end of the three years and it became obvious that I would need to convert to part-time study and finance the rest of the PhD through paid work. It is not unusual for arts and social science Research Students to take more than three years to complete the PhD; and it took me five years from start to finish.

Work

I managed to find part-time administrative work at the University of Leeds. This proved to be ideal as the location was only a five-minute walk from my academic office – no excuse not to do that research. The pay was also about the same as my yearly bursary, which ensured that my partner and I were equipped to survive financially, as he was working full-time. In fact, after I'd been in my part-time job for a year, we decided to settle in Leeds and buy a house. The part-time job made this possible.

The Research Culture

The post was to provide administrative support for Postgraduate Students to enhance the postgraduate students' university experiences. It was perfect because it was undemanding academically, but very sociable, involving numerous meetings as well as organising social events. I met a lot of other research postgraduates through the job and soon became aware of the advantages of studying in an 'old' university that has a history of research and an established research culture, something that was lacking in the 'new' metropolitan university where I was studying. For example, in the first three years, while I was working on the PhD full-time, I shared an office with lecturers in the social science department, which meant frequent interruptions from other members of staff and students and lead to lapses of concentration. However, at the establishment where I worked, I was interested to hear that science PhD students have a much more structured experience of research in the lab and meet their supervisor on an almost daily basis. In comparison, doing a PhD within the arts and social science area is often a lonely experience. The lack of research culture within my department also meant there was few opportunities to discuss research with colleagues or to present papers, (although other departments were aiming to develop this culture.) In fact, I often felt isolated in my tenth floor office. Thus, the perception of academics in ivory towers rang true for me. The job, therefore, provided me with a new group of colleagues and friends, with whom I had contact with on a weekly basis, which was extremely important to my self-identity. In a way, I felt like I had rejoined society. I also picked up new skills in computing as well as organisational competencies from the job that benefited my academic work. My employers also gained an administrator with first hand experience of studying for a PhD and taught postgraduate studies.

Off to Work I Go

The physical separation between my two types of work allowed me to step from the PhD to the paid work fairly easily. At the University of Leeds I was able to assume a different persona, put on a different hat and even wore smarter clothes on my 'work' days. It was extremely important that the administrative role did not interfere with my PhD and having that distance helped this. The job also required some evening work, which meant that I could do more work on the PhD during the day. This suited me because I could concentrate on the PhD in the mornings, a time when I worked better academically. However, it did lead to twelve or thirteen hour long days which were extremely tiring. I often found it difficult to sleep when I got home after an evening meeting. This was irritating because I knew I had to get up early the next morning and concentrate on the academic work.

There are also disadvantages in going straight from academic work to the administrative role; you don't get a break and tend to eat lunch at your computer, which is not good for the stress levels. There was a period of six months when the job became demanding and taxing. During this time I found that the work was taking up valuable PhD 'head space' which I resented. This was a stressful time and I coped by trying to keep a strict time division between the job and the PhD. I didn't have much time or energy for anything else, and it adversely affected my relationship and family life. My partner said that I was very difficult to live with during this time because I was on a very short fuse. His emotional and financial support throughout the five years was essential and I would never have completed it without him.

The other big disadvantage of doing a PhD part-time is that you have to cut off from academic work just when you are getting into it. For instance, when you are in the middle of writing a chapter, before you can begin from where you left off, you have to read everything you have written so far. This involves a high level of concentration and absorption in the work, if you only have a few hours each day to do this it means that your progress is frustratingly slow. In fact I found that everything took longer than expected.

During the two years I was working part-time, my supervisory meetings with my two supervisors became much less frequent but more structured. I received written feedback on chapters I had composed which was extremely useful. Whilst I met my first supervisor every four weeks, my second supervisors' office was at a different campus and meetings were more difficult. In fact the three of us only met as a team once. Working part-time also means that you have less flexibility and available time to meet and discuss your research. I found that I was unable to attend research seminars because of meetings and other paid work engagements. It would have been more beneficial to discuss my work face-to-face with my supervisors and also with other researchers working in the area. The need for a research forum to discuss on-going research in a supportive environment is important.

The Final Hurdle

The final six months became extremely demanding and juggling the job with the academic work was tough. I was fortunate because my employer is generous with holidays and I used those weeks to work on the PhD. However, this limits time to spend with your partner, family and friends and you become almost hermit-like. You really rely on people's understanding and I was very fortunate to have some fantastic supporters on the sidelines encouraging me to the end. I perhaps wasn't as committed to the job during this time, but as I mainly organised my own work schedule, I think, and I hope, that this went unnoticed.

Generally I would say that working part-time enhanced my PhD experience, because I was extremely isolated as a full-time Research Student. However, the stress of juggling two roles, particularly if they are demanding, can be detrimental to your well-being. In the end though, I'd say that getting the PhD was definitely worth it.

In Brief

- Combining employment with study has many financial benefits. I was able to buy a house.

- Academic office sharing can be distracting and destructive.

- Research forums provide good sources of feedback that can be utilised when the supervisor is unavailable.

- Family life can easily be affected by the pressures of study.

To PhD. or not To PhD?

Antonia Dodds

Selecting part-time PhD study for financial reasons, Antonia balances employment with social science research for a doctorate.

In the Beginning

I'd always pictured myself doing a research degree. This idea didn't take concrete shape until, after several years out of academia, I found myself back at university and working towards a Masters: a full-time Masters. A Masters financed by a University bursary and by my savings. The course had a high taught component. All in all, It was a thoroughly enjoyable experience and one which planted the bulbs of the PhD. However, funding for the PhD was an entirely different packet of seeds.

Money Money Money

I knew that financing the research would be exceptionally problematic. I failed to gain either Research Council or University funding. Unluckily for me, the year I applied, my University decided to cut the number of PhD scholarships it offered by two-thirds – the scholarships subsequently went back up the following year. Rather than curb my good intentions and reapply for funding, I decided that I would rather start part-time than not start at all. If I didn't do it then, there was a high possibility that I never would. Another factor pulled me in the direction of part-time study; the part-time fees at my institution were substantially lower than the full-time fees. (Although I have to point out, that this is no longer the case.) I also trusted that I would find a suitable job before my savings evaporated. I therefore embarked on the part-time PhD by default; I would have preferred to do it full-time.

In at the Deep End

The PhD began, and so did I – tired. I'd worked solidly in the gap between finishing the Masters and starting the course and this wasn't the ideal scenario. To register part-time and fulfil University requirements, I also had to trawl through the rigmarole of signing on at the DHSS, although I knew that I wouldn't be eligible. I was praying that a part-time job would turn up as I dreaded the wrath of sporadic temping and language teaching throughout summer. Departmental academic tutoring was also a definite 'No'. It's too inconsistent to provide a reliable income. A 'regular' part-time job appeared to provide the solution: I wouldn't always be living hand-to-mouth, and it would be convenient if I could find work in the University. Luck filtered through and in January, I filled the second university administration position that I applied for. Thankfully, my job is a permanent contract and is exactly half-time. I recall thinking that it might get me through the whole PhD. Three years later, I'm still doing it.

Part-Time Perks

What are the advantages of studying part-time? Well, without the option, I wouldn't be here in the first place. And depending on my frame of mind, that can also comprise the main disadvantage. In short, it provides a framework and helps overcome the isolation that often walks alongside PhD study. Two and a half days of paid work per week builds a structure to my time that otherwise wouldn't exist. As the number of academic contact hours I have is low, I aim to treat the PhD like another aspect of employment and work nine-to-five (or ten-to-six.) My office is busy, and my colleagues amiable, so the administration work provides the human contact that can often be lacking as research in the Social Sciences and Arts can be exceptionally isolating. I suspect that, if I were full-time, I would complain of being isolated. My situation does not, however, lend itself well to providing contact with people who are in the same situation as myself.

Hard Work

Perhaps, if I were working full time, I would desire a more demanding job. Nonetheless, I'm depositing in my 'bank' of skills – and one would hope that these might be useful when applying for full-time jobs, whether in academia or in administration. Being part of the admin. team has other, numerous advantages. I have met a far greater number of academics from various departments and have a broader understanding of the university than if I were just a research student. Also, within the job market, I am still a player. Furthering my career and qualifications has not meant four years 'out'.

An easier job (one for which I am over-qualified) has been a mixed blessing. I am not too tired to study; the work remains reasonably varied and whilst it may be under-stimulating at times, I mostly enjoy it. The location is a massive advantage. I have no excuse not to pop into the library after work, and if I need to swap my hours around for PhD reasons, then it is fairly easy to do so. Academically, my supervisors expect a reasonable amount of work from me. I'm content with the amount I see them (although I know that this varies hugely across the spectrum) and I have the same access to facilities as a full-time students. Moreover, it releases some of the pressure. I would not enjoy having to work a substantial number of hours a week on top of full-time study.

And what are the disadvantages? Foremost, it has to be the extra demands involved in juggling two jobs. The hours are less of a problem; whereas having to hold twice the amount of information in my head, and having to move perpetually between the two very different spheres of work can be challenging. It is also difficult to get immersed in academic study - say if I'm writing - as I'm always having to stop to go and head back to my paid job. Employment can make attendance at seminars difficult, as I always have to clock-watch, and I don't want to move my work hours around more than is necessary. Attending conferences means swapping days around, or taking holiday. So far it's meant that I can't teach in the department (which is pretty well necessary for an academic career) as I'm aware that teaching would 'wipe out' maybe two days a week, leaving me little time for my own research. Sometimes I enjoy the contrast of spending one day in a busy office, and the next in a quiet library/academic room, but at other times I find it difficult to adjust from one to the other. It can be hard to fit in fieldwork or use other library facilities. Doing this often requires that I use up holiday allowances, which means I don't have much in the way of 'real' holiday. I have on occasion had to change my research plan because of not being able to take several months off at a stretch.

Part Time Blues

The other main disadvantage is that the part-time PhD is much more lengthy. When I started, part-time PhDs were officially between four and six years; they've now increased to eight. This means that you're looking at a proportionately larger chunk of student life. I don't have much money and can't afford a mortgage – this can feel like I am putting my life on hold, especially when I compare my situation with peers who are climbing the career ladder. It also means that the various stages of the PhD last much longer. In my experience, the PhD has come together during the last few months, with significant ups and downs en route. Being a part-timer means that these exaggerated periods are greater, and the sense of floundering around in the swamp of academic uncertainty is with me for longer than if I was studying full-time.

I also find that I don't have an equivalent peer-group to measure myself against in terms of academic progress. Those that I started with are now finishing, which can cause me to feel left behind, in spite of the fact that I know this comparison is inappropriate. The habitual complaint of academic isolationism is compounded by the fact that I know very few other part-time PhD students. Those who do study in the same mode as me are usually in a different situation, i.e. were full-time but are now part-time as their funding has run out, or they already have academic jobs.

Financially, I'm worse off than those who received funding, (although I do have a minuscule pension, which funded PhDs don't) and part-time students are technically not eligible for student railcards and exemption from council tax. Any extra work that I do - such as teaching - is taxed, as my income is taxable, unlike a grant. Refusal of funding did nothing to aid academic self-esteem, which can be an ongoing crisis point in postgraduate study at the best of times. There can also be a tendency to see the paid job as my primary identity, and the PhD as a secondary (and therefore less important) identity, which is not beneficial for either myself or my research.

P.M.A. (Positive Mental Attitude)

But like so much else in life, part-time experiences depend heavily on mental attitude. When the PhD is not going well, there is a tendency to get stuck in a vicious circle of negativity. When it's falling into place, or I am maintaining a more positive mental attitude, I greatly enjoy the variety in my life. The qualities you need to get through any PhD are determination, motivation and self-belief, and that is never as true as when undertaking part-time study.

In conclusion

- Part-time study provided an economical solution to deferring my studies.

- Paid employment can provide a invaluable source of social contact and allow the student to remain an active player within the job market.

- Part-time students are often exempt from government financial aid such as tax relief.

- A positive approach is essential to success.

I Cyborg

Katherine Sargant

Katherine combined caring for her infant son with part-time,
taught postgraduate study. She has since had to suspend her
studies until a more suitable time arises.

Why cyborg you may ask? Well a cyborg is an apparently tame
chimera; that is a monster made up of differing parts. For a
cyborg, these parts are both mechanical and biological, and
being a part-time student of any subject suggests that you are a
multiplicity of things. But being a part-time student of Science
and Technology Studies, for me, invariably means that I become
the cyborg; and apparently not always so tame...

October of my first year: I choose to study just one of the six
units I'll need to complete in the following two, plus a
dissertation. Fifteen years on and I'm a student again. It's
amazing, and so very different to anything I've encountered
before. I feel welcome and supported, if rather unconfident and
fazed by the rabbit warren of a campus. The university system in
many ways becomes the mechanical part of my existence; I have
to perform and deliver to deadlines but the experiences are very
human. Yet there are other, more demanding parts to my person
- not least my three month old son...

Cyborg Mum

So off I go to my once weekly seminar, having left my son at the
university crèche. Oh, what joy! Oh, what confusion... I soon
discover that the part of my brain designated for understanding
exciting new ideas is the very part that constantly monitors the
well-being of my son; whether he's present or not. First
problem: learning to switch from one set of cybernetic feedback
loops to another. I need an 'or gate'. In time this becomes
much easier.

Switching off to Baby

Initially, switching off to baby is a physical impossibility. Every two to three hours, my two distinct bodily swellings flip back the 'on' switch. As the seminar develops, so does my son's hunger. By tea break, I'm ready to burst. I dash to the loo and then to my son for a quick top up. Needless to say, he, and I are both relieved - the downside being that during my first term, I never get to chat casually with the other students. But as he moves on to solids, so do I. The whole course becomes much more tangible, options open up, confidence is built, and a few friendships begin to form.

The First Essay

Christmas is spent crafting my first 5000 word essay. This is hard work - and The Cyborg makes her debut appearance. Locking myself away for long enough periods to think clearly is a definite challenge. My partner becomes a first-time, full-time father. And I become a milking machine. Remembering to drink enough is no the longer a problem. I consume endless nourishing warm beverages and type in my fingerless mitts, (the ancient central heating fails to reach me in my so called office.) But the end product is worthwhile and the process reintroduces me to the concision of academic writing.

Time Team

January comes and decisions have to be made - which course? When do I do it? The essay writing has unearthed the biggest logistical problem of all: my utter lack of flexible time. They say you can always create time. It is not until the summer that I realise what they don't tell you: something else will always come along and vacuum it up again.

My decision? Get the units out of the way and then do my essays. That ensures my reading is not overloaded. I decide to take two units in the second term, one of which the lectures are in the evening. This cuts the monetory cost of child-care and puts fathering firmly back on the agenda. The summer term is spent writing and grafting for these courses and in July, I take a two week intensive course. By my second year, there's only two units and a dissertation left to tackle. I also have a new group of very supportive friends, including a few tried and tested baby-sitters. Reading up and figuring out what I'm going to be able to research and write about consumes most of my October. As it happens, definitely more by luck than design, my last two essays and the dissertation form consecutive chapters to a rather theoretical thesis. No interviews. No ethnographies. Just my personal phenomenological research. (Phenomenology being the root of existentialism. It's about our Being-in-the-world - *our existence* - pertinent to my interests and the foundation of techno-science studies.) And now I just can't stop reading Heidegger. For the most part, people are fascinated - but confused, or more often amused by what I'm blathering on about. All those different bio-mechanical parts are beginning to integrate. *The cyborg caterpillar is pupating...*

The Technical Hitch

What about the first summer to be vacuumed? I'm starting a two-week intensive course entitled: *New Approaches to University Teaching*. 'Just up my street', I think, an ex-teacher honing my academic skills. No problem! The first week runs without a hitch - an agreeable group of people dotted with some interesting seminars and hard work late into the night. I'm doing fine - until Friday. What I have not bargained on getting is the worst case of Montezuma's Revenge I have ever experienced! We go down with it as a family, sorry, an *extended* family. I draft extra help in the form of my elderly parents. In turn, they too became extra work. The bug ensures that I miss most of the second week. I do, however, manage to crawl in for the last day and do my final 'performance' piece, rather off the cuff, to the judging group audience and video camera. I still can't watch that tape - the mere thought of it makes me queasy.

On the Mend

So the summer holidays are spent recovering. The weight has dropped off through illness and feeding my son. I have to rapidly wean him off me. I think it's more traumatic for me than for him. He voraciously takes to toddler foods and I'm feeling free. (So I think.) January passes and my old self eventually slips back into me - although the essay writing has come to an abrupt and nasty standstill.

Bug Free

January of the New Millennium: a time for resolutions? I carefully timetable each week between January and September – I am the epitome of organisation. But my son has different ideas. At eighteen months of age, he decides to anticipate being two. Battle ensues. Wrestling a budding two-year-old into clothes he fitted into last week is like decorating a bungee-jumping Christmas tree. Life becomes a series of, almost but not quite, *events*. Time as a concept evaporates...

I'm saved during the first five weeks by a departmental glitch that melts my ten-week unit into a five-week frolic, (complete with the occasional research method.) The course was planned to be a workshop, but with a registry of just two students, this intention quickly evaporates. In the end, we receive a tailor made affair, focusing on the 'doing' of a research dissertation.

System Overload

By March, I have to have a break. I'm lucky enough to have the spare cash and time for a short holiday with a friend in Florida.

Bliss!

After whirling through the heart of various tornadoes – the system gradually falls behind me. I can settle down at home. Routines emerge, research and essays are planned. It's certainly no tornado-toddler free zone, but I've acquired the vitality to stay on course. Only five months left and 25,000 words to draft on four different subjects. Without a timetable for us all to stick to, it'll be virtually impossible.

And the Rest?

All day Monday, and every Thursday morning, I'm a mum. I do the laundry, go to Sainsburys and complete the myriad of household chores. Every other weekend I take a break - if I'm on schedule. Otherwise, I work. I still enjoy what I'm doing, but it's invariably tough. I pay masses of attention to my son's needs, but my adult relationships are suffering; especially with my partner. There are moments of over-focusing on work. So at times I'm monstrous. Though, without his support, it would not be practically possible. His indifference, (as I sometimes see it) to both me and my work, keeps me from digressions and explanations. In fact, I recently discovered, he has a fear and loathing of intense concentration - it leaves him fatigued. Watching me work so hard is wearing him out as much as watching out for our son.

Mechanical Production

My cyborg self is now a complex mechanism for churning thoughts into text. The mechanical and biological are indistinguishable, but not quite fused. The summer months each produce an essay. September 9th is, *The Big One*: the final dissertation - I know I have to make the effort. Everyone is feeling the fatigue, and I'm submerged in guilt for the amount of time my son had spent at the crèche. So when we fly out of Heathrow airport for two weeks walking in Finnish Lapland - it's total bliss. Again. We have to learn to communicate, to work as a close team. The holiday is just what we need.

Having got into such a successful routine of work over the summer, I decide to embark upon a PhD. October comes and I try to jump back onto the merry-go-round. This time, I believe I'm going to balance the time better between study and family.

I fail.

We all get the usual October bug, and I can no longer hold my balance. We all battle on with the bug until December, then it's Crunch Time. No work complete and my academic focus having all but disappeared, I decide to suspend my studies.

System Reload

Giving up is never a failure. It is usually common sense coming into focus, before another opportunity takes you off to Never-Never-Again-Land. I continue to tinker with various ideas; waiting for funding to fall into place. The most useful things I have extracted from my experience of being a part-time post-grad are the 'human' effects. Discovering my own abilities is one thing. But understanding the importance of the people bound up in my life, especially in academia, has been essential. I'm also learning how important it is to remain part of other people's lives.

Having another existence outside of study may at times be distracting, but it also keeps me sane. A two year old, like most grown-ups, can be a devil or an angel. Playing fifty-two-card pick-up with the contents of your files is annoying, but seeing him desperately trying to tidy them up is special. Moments like this keep my feet firmly planted in relative values. What might be, and what really is important are often two separate things. Support comes from many diverse places, and remaining receptive to this support is essential.

Rules of the Cyborg

So what are the rules, if any? This cyborg is a part-time student, with a family. A famous sci-fi writer, Isaac Asimov*, once stated:

1. A robot may not injure a human being or through inaction allow a human being to come to harm.

2. A robot must obey the orders given to it by human beings except where such orders would conflict with the first law.

3. A robot must protect its own existence so long as such protection does not conflict with the first or second law.

You may not wish to become a cyborg, and no one would welcome being a robot. But in my case, these rules still apply.

----

* "I Cyborg" is a reverential reference to "I Robot" by Isaac Asimov [1950]. In this book amongst his many others about robots, robotics and humans he explores and develops his three laws of robotics; as referenced here.

The Succinct Cyborg

- Combining caring for a very young child and studying can be an ominous mix of conflicting emotions.

- Near perfect organisation is the only way to make it possible, although life can (and will) throw out the unexpected.

- Rest breaks are essential to restore vitality, but suspending study is sometimes the only viable option.

The Good, the Bad and the Ugly

Christopher Clark
Christopher is currently studying towards a PhD.

I started my PhD in 1993 and am due to submit my thesis within the next twelve months. In many ways, the whole experience has been nothing short of extreme – the good and the bad always inextricably entwined. Having completed a course that was three quarters practical, I hadn't a clue of what a PhD entailed. It took a move to a second university and a change of supervisor to find out.

Problems with my original supervisor were evident from the start – but with few initial ideas of what to expect, I didn't realise the extent of the difficulties. Moreover, most of my fellow students were also dissatisfied with their supervisors. Such problems comprised a large part of research students' conversations.

Trouble Ahead

My supervisor was unable to teach or guide me in a way that was beneficial. He would act in a 'professional' manner, but was unable to meet me at my level – he could only beckon from where he was standing. Constant reminders were given that my writing was not up to the required standard, but insufficient advice offered about how to improve it. Academic conventions can only appear obvious once you have learnt them. He also lacked what I now believe to be one of the most important attributes of a supervisor: interpersonal skills - the ability to encourage and show belief in my abilities to undertake the research. A PhD is inherently isolating, so positive contact with others is essential.

The problems didn't halt there. I was in a department that had very little experience of research students. No great thought had

The problems didn't halt there. I was in a department that had very little experience of research students. No great thought had been given to the type of the research that PhD students could undertake. No agreed strategy existed as to how research degrees that combined practical and theoretical work could be undertaken. There was no formal provision for upgrading from M.Phil. to PhD status, unlike other departments that had 'upgrade' boards. Little consideration had been given to students like myself who had come to university via art school and needed to make a transition to the academic environment. Training courses were available, but not in my field.

Within my department, energies were focussed on starting up taught MA courses. Strategies were devised to pull in new research students rather than improve the existing provisions. Lack of progress was attributed to the supposed individual inadequacies of the postgraduate students. We were too slow. Too young. We found the research too hard. Should the department have enrolled students that they believed to lack the required time, energy and commitment to attain the necessary standard?

The New University Environment

Having been in art school as opposed to university, this new environment appeared cold and alienating. Used to being submerged in the mess that is part of the package of most art colleges, I found university life controlled, sterile and uninviting. The buildings and their contents were vastly different and the whole language and social conventions were entirely new to me. Whilst art schools have hierarchies, the university hierarchies were more graduated and complex and it took time to learn the unwritten social norms. Some of the more obscure academic language and debates were virtually incomprehensible. This gave way to my current belief in the importance of ethics in academia. I feel language should be used as a tool for progressive education rather than to inflate the academics' egos or to produce more papers and books to meet research outcomes.

The Flip Side

In many ways, I did gain from the department. There was extensive teaching available and substantial help with practical work and professional development. However, after four years of university without an upgrade, I realised that it was never going to happen. (Indeed I bumped into an ex fellow student who was still an M.Phil. registration after seven years.)

Having made the decision to transfer, I flicked through the graduate guide to check for the institutions that had supervisors in my field. With my choice narrowed to six, I rang the potentials and spoke to the supervisors. After one aborted interview in London, (the department felt they did not have the necessary resources to support me) I was accepted at my current university. This has been a redeeming experience. I now have a supervisor that any student would wish for – someone who is thoughtful, pragmatic, supportive and most importantly, can provide help according to my stage of development. She spends no more time with me than my first supervisor, but boosts my confidence, shows interest in my work and conveys her belief in my ability to do it. The pastoral angle has been the key: a student will need their supervisor less if their confidence in their own abilities is raised.

Progression

My PhD initially began as part theory and part practice. After six months at a new university, I ditched the practice as I found working between the two artificial and difficult. Combining both meant contextualising my own work against that of world famous artists – this was absurd. Their roots and realities are so removed from mine that comparing them at this level is deeply problematic. Difficulties with PhDs in Art Practice generally seem to be insufficiently discussed. How can they be distinguished from an MA or PhD in Fine Art, for example? Should the subject squeeze itself into something with an academic tradition? I began my course as a 'hard-nosed' career decision. I had wanted to teach for a long time - it seemed like a good career option for an artist as opposed to dancing attendant on the vagaries of galleries and the art market.

Through undertaking the research I have learned an enormous amount, often in areas that could not have been envisaged. I have been both excited and constrained by the rigours of academic training. I have gained greatly in learning to read and evaluate material, think more deeply and become more articulate and discriminating. Immersion in academia has given me a deeper experience of the world, and, as a lecturer, I have gained confidence through teaching part-time throughout my research.

At times, disappointment has plagued me. PhD study can be mundane. I carried many romantic fantasies about intellectual circles after reading Sartre and De Beauvior as a teenager. And university life was more prosaic than this. My research has been discussed with others, but as I am the only person involved in it, these conversations are few and far between. Friends from other disciplines read my work and offer helpful comment – something for which I am grateful as I usually only discuss formal aspects of my work with my supervisor.

And the Rest of My Life?

It's an exhausting task trying to balance the various facets of my life with my PhD. Paid work, research, working life and social life do not slot together easily. Achieving this balance, has, and still is a day by day (and often minute by minute) struggle. Ironically, it has only been since I gained a fractional learning post, (and transferred to a new university) that my research has taken a turn for the better. A permanent employment contract has boosted my self-esteem, granted me a routine and structure around which to fit my research and had the added advantage of providing a steady and adequate income.

Coping

Without mention of isolation and loneliness – this chapter would not be complete. The first few years were awash with distress due to the lack of timetable and formal structure. I was floating with few anchors and everything I added to steady my life pulled me away from my research. A constant daily struggle ensued: did I undertake the research, and if so, was I ready to tackle the feeling of loneliness that this usually brought? Or do I do something social and be faced with the anxiety of putting the PhD off? It is hard to pull yourself out of bed in the morning knowing that you only have your research to occupy your day. Moreover, through working alone in a studio for three years, I associated a certain type of isolation with academic study. With art pieces, grabbing people to discuss and look at your work is easy – it only takes a short time and people generally love seeing 'live' work. Art also has a physical presence that you can respond to and which can makes you feel alive. Writing has fewer of these qualities. It can, at a distance, lie inert on the page.

Time-tabling my life became an essential factor in combating this feeling of isolation. On the days that I was doing research, I ensured that I was meeting someone or doing something different for lunch or in the evening to divide the time and make it manageable. The support, comradeship and shared social lives of friends doing research became crucial. I also benefited from the university's counselling service. Once-weekly, I offloaded the tensions of what appeared to be an impossible situation. Meditation practice, both on and off the cushion, has also proved to be another anchor.

Over time, I have realised that the research has a life and momentum of its own; regardless of how hard I work or how tense I become. At times it's hard to stand at a distance and trust that it will evolve in its own time, but I know that I can only work with it and coax it along.

In Brief

- Switching to a new university gave my study renewed direction and vigour.

- For art an ex art college student, the university environment seemed 'sterile' and a process of adjustment had to occur. Counselling proved beneficial.

- Routine was integral to ensuring a social and academic balance.

The Agony and Ecstasy of Part Time Study

Scott Holtham
A teacher, Scott has just completed a Masters degree in Literature with the Open University.

I have always admired those people who possess the motivation and drive to study in difficult circumstances. The single parent who studies for a doctorate whilst holding down a demanding job and attending to the needs of three young children. The surgeon who writes a scholarly work on some long-forgotten nineteenth-century author, rising every morning at 5am to fit in a few hours work before. . . before *work*. I am not one of these people. I do not pursue my literary studies in a garret. I do not spend twelve hours a day flexing my muscles and numbing my mind in some brutal, manual labour-intensive job. No, my life is easy and my domestic life supportive. Sure, I work full-time. I work as a teacher. It is a demanding job and to be honest, settling down on a weekday evening for two hours with an 800 page novel or some terse tome of criticism is not always attractive. But something propels me on, some deep, inner feeling keeps me studying for the MA. Well, I like studying, if only in the most dilettante of ways. It's a need that demands satisfaction.

The Return to Education

Fifteen years after finishing my first degree - and having sent off for many university postgraduate prospectuses throughout that period with a vague intention of doing something at MA level - I finally took the plunge and registered for an Open University part-time MA in Literature in August 1997. The course of study is planned to run over three years, though some students – with difficulty I may say – finish it within two. I liked the way the O.U. arranges its academic year to run from February to October. Working as a secondary school teacher, I knew that the holidays would be good insurance against exhaustion, apathy and procrastination – the enemies I feared that would try and stop me from studying while also working in a full-time job.

There are obviously many reasons why people choose to study for a part-time higher degree. I had initially registered for a professionally orientated degree with the O.U. This decision, however, was made with the head and not with the heart. I reasoned that such a qualification might be a sensible thing to work for. But for me, 'being sensible' has never been a personal quality in much supply. I teach English – you know, poetry, novels, that kind of thing – my heart said 'Forget the career stuff, do Eighteenth-century Literature instead.' I switched courses. I knew my only chance of success was to do something I had a passion for.

The Agonies of Self Doubt

Much mental agony and anguish followed registration. Self-doubt and worry about being able to do the course properly hounded me for the five months leading up to the start. Several times I came close to cancelling my enrolment. But looking over the O.U. course structure was a great comfort in my times of woe. A postgraduate foundation course in the first year was recommended as a good way of easing back into higher education. Three essays, gradually increasing in length, were expected in the first year. And this course required only about eight hours study a week rather than the more daunting fourteen recommended for a full course. This, plus a few tutorials, seemed manageable for even my fickle ways of studying. Yet how do I describe the frisson of panic that ran through me when, sometime after I had paid my fee, I reread the course details and discovered that a three-hour examination would be the concluding unit to the course? How could I have missed such an incredibly important detail? Okay, so I set exams all the time – but I had not *sat* one since 1984. Well, it would have to be done. I was always going on about exam technique to my classes wasn't I? Now we would see if I could practise what I preached.

When the study pack arrived in the January of 1997 I was full of enthusiasm and sprang into action immediately. I knew that capitalising on this initial excitement would 'buy' me time later on when I would have more pressing concerns at work. Time management is an essential skill for the part-time student. If you want to get the best out of the course, leaving things to the last minute is simply not an option. And for an MA essay, particularly in literature, it just isn't possible to waffle your way to a high mark. There is no escaping the diligence required at this level of scholarship. Studying literature means plenty of reading – and eighteenth-century authors clearly wrote for people with time on their hands. Now I sigh with relief when I set about reading a book that is only a mere 500 pages long.

My first essay took much longer than necessary. It was only supposed to be 1500 words but it took me hours, days, to draft and redraft. I also fell into the trap of convincing myself that it was impossible to address the issue in question in fewer than 2000 words. My paper was returned thoroughly annotated and I was flattered to receive a mark just under distinction. I was penalised for excessive length – a salutary lesson in the necessity of getting to the point.

Essay writing became easier as the course progressed, but as the exam approached I became anxious about my tendency to endlessly rework. Would I be able to get it right first time in the exam? Exam nerves haunted me in a way I had never experienced in the cavalier days of my youth. I practised writing 'under exam conditions' but I have never been good at fooling myself in this way. To my, maybe mistaken, way of thinking, the only way to prepare for an exam is by doing the thing. When the time came, my problem lay not in knowing how to express myself concisely but in the physical process of writing the answer down. I rarely use a pen for much more than writing the odd cheque or marking students' work at school – neither of which requires the physical dexterity essay writing demands. Half way through the three-hour exam, with one essay done and another to be begun, my right hand suddenly developed arthritic symptoms and reduced my writing speed to a snail's pace. The ideas were queuing up to be put down, but I was at the mercy of my aching fingers. If exam practice is useful in any sense it is for this – get used to writing for a long time with a pen!

Intuitive Insights

What has been incredible is the extent to which I have become reliant on my subconscious. The part-time postgraduate cannot afford to restrict his or her studies to something done behind a desk. Many of my essay plans and insights into a scholar's argument have come to me at 3am, in the shower, or standing in assembly at school. I have to keep small notepads all over the house just in case I have an idea that needs to be put down before I forget it. Related to this is the need to be organised. I am notoriously messy with everyday household admin like bills, bank statements and so on. Such a haphazard approach is not recommended for the budding scholar. I write all essays on the PC but take notes on 8 by 5 index cards. I find the size of the card forces me to be concise in note-taking and to avoid copying lengthy and usually unnecessary chunks out of books and journals.

Having the use of a computer has been essential. Although the hand-written essay, I believe, demands a tighter mental discipline, I have always found 'writer's block' to be a major obstacle to getting anything down on paper. With the word processor I can get stuck in without having to worry about where to start, getting the right phrasing or getting things wrong. I can just *write*. Once I feel I have got close to the word limit, I can set about hacking away the dross and waffle. The MA essay also requires much closer attention to the conventions of recording bibliographic sources. I have saved much time through recording references as I have come about them rather than leaving them all to the last minute. Internet access has also been very useful for checking the stock of library catalogues and ordering books in advance. The working part-timer needs all the help he or she can get.

I have already mentioned that my initial fear of taking up studying again was to fall prey to lethargy and prevarication. As it turned out, the biggest problem facing the part-time student is compromise: and compromise produces guilt: the guilt of pursuing superfluous pleasures in one's spare time. Over the past two years I have deliberately limited my reading to books relevant to my course. But my reading tastes are wide and varied and going into any bookshop now produces feelings of excitement and frustration in equal measure. For one week last summer I forced myself to take a holiday from the eighteenth century. This was an opportunity to indulge a whim I'd been nurturing for a few American novels. I bought several books by Bellow, Hemingway and Capote and wallowed in the pleasure of reading for its own sake. Thoroughly satisfied, I could return to my studies.

But the effect of postgraduate part-time study on my life cannot be overestimated. Once upon a time I used school holidays for catching up on marking, sorting out school admin and going to the cinema. These days I take more marking home during the week, forget the admin and forget about going to the cinema. I have found that the feeling of guilt seeps into all areas of one's life. My professional life has occasionally compromised my study time but I have also allowed my studies to marginalise concerns at work. Some people I know are very good at keeping the two separate, or diligently prioritise work before study. I have not always been successful in this respect.

What will I do when I have finished? My tutor asked me recently if I'd given any thought to a PhD. That would mean another five years of self-denial. Am I wrong in thinking that the part-time student must have a masochistic streak? A large part of me will be sad to stop studying. Over the last year I have read twelve novels from the eighteenth century, one of which was Richardson's *Clarissa* that left me half-crazy. I enjoyed all of them and I enjoyed all the attendant lit crit. I know that if it had not been for the focussed study demanded from the MA I would never have read any of those books so diligently, would never have learnt so much about them and the time they were written in. How will I justify sitting in the Humanities Reading Room of the British Library every Saturday when my thesis is complete? I'll miss the quiet, purposeful atmosphere and the incredibly comfortable leather desk chairs. But think of all those books and films I'll be able to catch up on! Ah, the agony and ecstasy of being a part-time student.

Top Tips

- Foundation courses can help rebuild academic confidence after years 'out'.

- Exams are daunting, but practice is essential, especially in preparation for the physical demands of prolonged writing.

- Tools can ease the burden, such as idea notepads and word-processors.

Part Time Study: Part Time Life?

Tanya Richardson

Tanya is working through a part-time, taught Masters programme. Her employment within the same establishment remains her highest priority

My Course Specifics

I am currently mid-way through my second year of a two year part time taught combined Masters degree in Women's Studies and Sociology. It is fair to say, I have experienced the gamut of emotions about my studies over the last 18 months. I embarked on my MA with an abundance of enthusiasm and energy - not to mention some pretty high expectations. Some expectations have been realised and others not.

Work, Rest and Play

I came back to study having graduated 3 years earlier. I am lucky enough to have been employed part time (30 hours a week) by the University for the past 3 years and I guess I saw the combination of my working locally and my growing corporeal restlessness as the perfect opportunity to pursue further studies. It's unlikely that I would have applied for postgraduate study had I not had an extraordinarily supportive boss and colleague who enabled me to have flexible working hours/ days to accommodate shifting timetables.

Initially I found the transition back to 'school' somewhat stressful. The trials of finding time - in an already busy life schedule - for seminars, reading but more importantly, essay writing, are enormous. Some part-time students work in order to study, but for me, the studies needed to fit in around work and other commitments. I became aware quite early in the degree that for many postgraduate students the degree was the primary focus of their lives - at least for that year (or two). This perspective was reflected in the approach of some of the teaching staff. Changing timetables and the expectation that reading/ writing can be done at extremely short notice, implies that study should be *the,* or at least one of, the highest priorities in our lives.

Negotiating the time problem (shortage of it) has been no simple task, and while I am satisfied with my decisions and prioritising, I'm not really sure if I have entirely resolved it. I have at times felt resentful of giving up weekends to work, taking annual leave to write essays and generally working to full capacity - particularly at those times when the work is somewhat less than inspiring. But, I have to say, it has become a great deal easier, I adapted to this schedule over time.

Academic work is an all-consuming constant, there is always more you can read, more you can say and more you can think. For me, it has been paramount to acknowledge that the task is infinite but my time and energy is not. Hence, the compromise, or what I would rather refer to as the 'sanity saver', has been essential. Recognising the infinite nature of the pursuit of academic excellence and establishing realistic goals, differentiating what is possible - reasonable and enough to enable me to take from the course what I had hoped to achieve - and realising what is just mad. Without this I think I would have been a better student but certainly a less happy one. I had to remind myself that I should not beat myself up about not being as good as I maybe could have been.

I have needed to block out time and energy in order to maintain parts of my life. (I work to pay the rent, play sport to keep healthy, see friends to stay social/normal and a maintain a long-distance relationship) I feel these are necessary to achieve a level of happiness. These non-academic parts of my life have been, and continue to be, integral pieces which are neither necessary nor healthy to surrender for a Masters degree. I am not one to subscribe to the theory of accepting living hell for a longish period of time in order for some greater gain.

The Taught Masters

There are two aspects of a taught Masters degree that potential applicants might want to consider. First, the fact that many courses are split into taught modules brings with it issues that you would be less likely to encounter in postgraduate doctorate research. These issues include the limbo status of the taught MA student - being neither an undergraduate nor a fully realised/ recognised research student. It's an odd space to occupy in academia, feeling integrated into neither the undergrad nor the postgrad ranks. Status is often confusing and isolating, with the possible consequence of feeling yourself not to be a 'serious' postgraduate. Secondly, some taught (sometimes verging on spoon-feeding) courses, leave limited intellectual space (and often support) to explore your own research interests - unless you are lucky enough to have a resident expert nearby with whom you have made positive contact.

Two Years Vs. One

I acknowledge the rising number of Masters students, many of whom are an overspill of undergraduates who use further degrees as a stop-gap to employment outside of academe. Combine this with the reality that many departments have limited resources and what we get is an inevitable mixture of those interested and those uninterested in pursuing an academic career path, and the institutions needing to spend their resources in the best places possible.

What a taught Masters degree has offered me over the last eighteen months is the opportunity to differentiate between what does and what does not interest me. This might be less important for somebody who has direction within a particular field - but I wanted to re-engage with studying without having a defined research interest. The taught Masters was the right decision. I'm unsure whether the evolution of my interests would have developed fully had I been studying full-time -

82

words like 'wood' and 'trees' leap to mind. Spread over two years, I have had the opportunity to reflect on my experience rather than become consumed by it, and worked actively to confine studying to just one part of my life. I can't help but feel that this perspective might well have been lost had I studied full time.

Advice for part-time students

1. *Reading group*, reading group, reading group, reading group. Have I mentioned reading group?

   One particular reading group proved to be my lifeline in my first year of study. As a part-timer, with limited contact time with tutors and other students, the academic experience can, I think, be essentially isolating. Early on, (i.e. the first two weeks) I set about selecting a couple of students from the core course who I felt that - from what little contact I had had with them - I could work closely with and generate interesting discussions. We established a group and met weekly. We usually had a meal and resolved any issues from the previous week's seminar, and looked ahead at the issues we might want to think about for the next one. The time was social and productive and worked very well for me as someone whose preferred learning style is interactive. Obviously people opt for different modules, so maintaining the same group might not be possible for many students, but I would definitely encourage all postgraduate and, particularly part-time, students to set up their own groups. It can prove an interesting way to explore working with other people - who will no doubt have their own agendas - and help you to discover the best uses of time. I feel it added depth to my courses.

2. *Keeping in contact* with the main department you are connected to is very important as a part-time student.

Unless you work particularly well in a vacuum, it is useful to make sure you are informed about open seminars, social events and that the departmental secretaries know your face. To get the most out of the department, feeling part can help you to avoid the isolation that can follow independent learning. Apart from anything else, it's nice to speak regularly to people who are also struggling with essays, deadlines, tutors, career plans etc....

Final thoughts

Once I abandoned my dreams of what the degree would bring me, I could get on with the serious business of creating spaces outside of seminars to get the most out of the courses. I realised early on that I work well in an interactive and lively environment and that isolated learning depresses and drains me. Having picked myself up from flagging motivation, I realised that the environment had at times made me painfully aware of where I do and do not belong. I am hoping that this second year will continue, (as it is thus far proving) to afford me the opportunity to explore my research interests with a supportive supervisor. I feel as though I need less guidance now than at the beginning of the course, but I have yet to tackle my dissertation. There is also that nagging question of what the hell I'll do with my weekends once it's over?!

Mission Impossible: Doing a Part Time PhD, (or Getting 200% out of 20%) - Is it Really Worth it?

Caroline Gatrell

Caroline combines motherhood with her post as a Teaching Fellow and part-time PhD studies

At the beginning of the year 2000, I read my horoscope for the forthcoming twelve months. It was predicted that I would be working on an important project, to which I would 'give 200%'. While, in general, I don't take the stars too much to heart, there was a ring of truth in these words. I thought immediately of my PhD. I am someone who takes commitment very seriously. I have always worked hard. The problem for me, however, as for all part-time students, is that I am currently combining several important projects, each of which seems to require 200% of my time and energy.

The Balancing Act

Where do I start? Well, firstly, I have an infant daughter (the main priority), to whom I try and give 200 percent. I combine motherhood with my work as a Teaching Fellow. Although my (part-time) paid work is undoubtedly interesting and fulfilling, there is always pressure to 'give greater' than the 60% for which I am contracted. This is in some respects self-imposed because, like all my colleagues, I try to provide as much support as possible to the students, who are themselves working under considerable pressure. Like me, most of them stand firmly in the middle of a balancing act between children, classes and careers.

My weekdays are shared between my daughter, my paid work and my PhD, to which I devote every Thursday. It does not take a genius to work out that this equates to only 20% of the working week, (leaving me 180% short if I need to give it 200%.) I am in my second year of study and have quite a way to go before completion. A *'how to juggle everything successfully and do a part-time PhD before breakfast...'* account would sound smug as I still have a long stretch ahead before I can trudge to the finish-line. However, I've had my ups and downs and learned some serious lessons along the way. These are worth sharing.

The Beginnings

When I registered as a PhD student, I was perhaps more complacent than I might have been about combining study with work and motherhood. I had already completed a part-time MBA, and gained a Distinction. I assumed that this would be an advantage - and in many ways it has proved to be an ideal foundation. Starting with the confidence that success brings, I discovered that the discipline imposed by the MBA deadlines had become a habit, and the concept of late-night study so familiar that it was almost routine. The MBA had honed my writing and research skills, and drastically improved my reading speeds. The more you read, the more quickly you digest the required information. In spite of my somewhat disciplinarian training, there have been still been aspects of PhD study for which I was not prepared in the slightest.

The Differences of a PhD

Doing a PhD is completely different from working through a taught degree programme. Defined 'stepping stones' are laid out in the latter for you to follow and you can skip through your journey with relative focus and direction. However, the flexibility of a PhD can be advantageous for part-time students. Those who combine study with families and careers will know that there are times when life throws out problems. Part-time students have the invaluable option to put their research 'on hold', returning at a later (and indeed quieter) date without having missed important course work and feeling behind in comparison with their colleagues.

However, tackling a major piece of research, for which you are solely responsible, is undeniably intimidating. On beginning my PhD, I felt daunted by the sheer scale of the work I was undertaking. Questions zipped through my mind: Where should I begin? How would I know when I had done enough? Would I ever settle on a suitable research question? My first three months as a PhD student were spent reading everything in sight - I had to decide upon that question. Anxiety brewed as the time slipped by - what good was the ability to read quickly, when I hadn't a clue what I was reading *for?* I had ideas, but I was torn between them. What I really craved to do was some original research on combining motherhood with career.

The Big Question

However, more self contained, straightforward (and less controversial) topics were on offer and my mind was awash with the intricacies of each. Phillips and Pugh (1994) in ' *How to Get A PhD'* state that Einstein did not formulate the theory of relativity in his PhD, but made *'a sensible contribution to Brownian motion theory'.* This advice left me despondent. The self contained topics, which may have been sensible, remained totally uninspiring. It was at this point that I had an influential meeting with a senior, female academic. She argued that, particularly for the part-time students, it is important to choose a subject that 'burns you up' in order to 'keep you going'. In the end, I chose this route. And, I have no regrets (though there has been a price to pay.

Choosing something significant has meant that my research is like a good novel - impossible to put down. Throughout the past twelve months, when dropping with tiredness after my day-time responsibilities, I have gathered the energy to return to my office. Even at night, I can move forward with my PhD.

Part-Time Problems

On reflection, I can't help but to wonder whether the challenges of starting out would have been less daunting had I chosen to study full-time. Most full time graduate students, even PhDs (especially those funded by ESRC), are obliged to undertake taught courses during their first year. These commitments take up a big chunk of time. Some students resent them. But major advantages can be gained from attending research training programmes. A good deal of practical, 'how to do research' material is offered to full time students in a neat package. Part-timers, on the other hand, often have no choice but to plough through the relevant texts by themselves. Elements they do not understand can remain blurry until their next supervision meeting. More importantly, those students who *are* able to attend research-training courses have a ready-made circle of colleagues, all struggling with the same concepts at the same time.

Supervision

Courses are designed so students can discuss their own work within the context of the general research topic. Therefore, making sure you choose a good supervisor is absolutely crucial. I am jointly supervised by two academics who both provide excellent support. We meet regularly (about once a month) and both are prepared to talk to me outside the official sessions if I need advice.

I have, however, learned that no matter how closely you work with your supervisors, there is no substitute for establishing a network of other students - even setting up regular meetings from time to time, if you can find people who are near enough geographically. In this respect, I obviously have an advantage as I am both a student and an employee within the same establishment, but even so, I was well into my first year of study before

a) I realised the benefits

b) That other students welcome the opportunity to discuss their research and the problems of doing a part-time PhD

Recently, I joined a 'PhD Pressure Group' established by women doing part-time PhDs. I have also become friends with two women who have just finished their (full-time) doctorates. Both have offered support, encouragement and advice. I also have the authority of those who have done it.

The Lows

Having experienced a mostly happy and successful first year, I suffered my first serious low during the second. It was other students, in addition to my supervisors, who encouraged me to resolve the situation and get back on track. My low was the most recent in a series of similar encounters, all of which relate to my choice of a controversial, contemporary subject. Here's what happened.

So far, I have presented my work in public on three occasions - audiences have responded emotionally, and occasionally with aggression. My first presentation consisted of a formal progress talk to a group of twenty other interdisciplinary PhD students. My presentation was the last of four, all of which had been followed by polite and constructive debate. My turn came, and it was as though, to quote one of the participants, I had 'lit the blue touch paper'. Two male students began shouting. The women in the room began shouting at them. Questioning the legitimacy of pieces of research about women's issues, they argued: "Why should there be a department of Women's Studies anyway?" This angered the women. One said "I feel sorry for you because you cannot undergo the experience of bearing children and you hate that." The PhD itself became irrelevant. Arguments ensued about whether career women should have babies at all, and whether Women's Studies is a legitimate subject.

On the second occasion, the reaction was similar. I was in Bradford, speaking to a group of fifteen new academics from all over UK. One male lecturer responded with the (serious) comment that mothers of small children ought not to work because they should be at home, breast-feeding. The validity of the research was questioned again by a female academic - she felt excluded, due to having no children of her own. While this may have been a legitimate point, I did wonder whether her feelings would have been so strong had the PhD been about rocket science. Another man compiled a list of words that he claimed were used in the presentation. He criticised them, because they were too 'emotive. I had read from a typescript and was able to compare his list of 'emotive' words against my notes. They were not there. I can only surmise that the man *himself* felt so emotional about the subject, that he imagined the existence of words I had never used.

I was shaken after these experiences, but I carried on with my PhD in private and put off presenting the work in public again until recently. The PhD is now more advanced with an initial 30,000 words written, and a pilot study of interviews with mothers and fathers successfully completed.

In October 1999, I presented some preliminary findings to a small group of senior academics, one of whom 'went off at the deep end'. This individual, whom I shall call Professor Smith, let it be known that he did not believe that women over 35 should give birth at all, and explained that he felt personally 'violated' by the area of concern. At one point in the discussion, Professor Smith actually asked whether I was pregnant myself. Although the others present were constructive and encouraging, Professor Smith's response to the PhD really 'got me down' and for the first time since I started, I stopped working on it altogether, and seriously wondered whether to give it up. My despondency was caused by the fact that as a part-time student, I am already trying to give 200% to each of a variety of commitments, without the added complication of attempting a PhD under such difficult circumstances.

Personal Sacrifices

As those who are doing this particular form of study will know, the price of doing a part-time higher degree bears a heavy personal cost. Since 1995, I have spent many nights burning the midnight oil, when I know I have to be up next morning to get my daughter ready for nursery and do a day's work. I have sacrificed all the hobbies I once enjoyed, and I no longer paint, read novels or take part in amateur dramatics. Although I try not to let study encroach on weekends, there have been Sundays when I have guiltily left my family to their own devices, while I spent a day in my office, working on the PhD. I have fought to balance my research with my paid work (which also involves evening working) as well as with (most importantly) ensuring that my daughter does not suffer as a result of my wish to study. After the most recent incident, I did find myself seriously asking the question: *"Is this worth it? Is the personal cost of doing a PhD part-time really worth it, if this is how people are going to behave?"*

The Extreme

Since I am writing this, you will guess that I decided to continue. I have considered why my research topic causes such extreme reactions. Evidence in the literature suggests that this may be because my PhD, although it does not claim to *be* a paradigm shift, probably *reflects* several, which is what makes it so contentious. The first paradigm shift may lie in the very fact that I am a woman doing a higher degree. In discussing the problems facing women PhD students, Phillips and Pugh describe academia as a traditionally male environment, which can *'allow prejudice to be manifested'* (1994:119). The second paradigm shift is the concept that women's issues have a place in what is generally recognised as 'knowledge' in the academic sense. As

Tanton (1994:12 - 13) points out: *'The content of what is taught (in higher education) is still (apart from in Women's Studies) largely as a result of male research on male subjects....'* The third paradigm, that of the research itself, represents a major social change. The benefits or otherwise of combining motherhood and profession are debated in many arenas. Significantly, despite equal opportunities legislation, a current policy document issued by the Institute of Directors states that *'It is a biological fact that it is women who give birth to children and are best equipped to look after them in the early years.'* (Malthouse 1997).

On the Up

Undoubtedly, a rational analysis of why my research is seen as so contentious within the public arena, has helped provide an explanation for what happened. However it must be also said that it was fellow students, as well as my supervisors, who motivated me to respond positively when I asked the question: *'Is this really worth it?'.* The student networks that I have formed over the past six months were a significant influence in giving me the confidence and determination to keep going when the disadvantages of continuing threatened to outweigh the benefits. I am pleased that this is the case because on reflection, I am still convinced that my topic is an important one, which *is* worth researching - even if it is controversial.

And Finally

It might be worth summing up the factors that have helped me get this far. For me, at least, it was important to choose a subject which mattered and which I believed to be important. So long as I get there in the end, it is possible that my work might make a contribution to improving the situation for career mothers. A good working relationship, and regular meetings with supervisors is central to a part-time PhD student, as is establishing networks with other students who know how you feel and who are experiencing the same pressures as you (if they can do it, so can you.) For those readers who are worried about how and where to find other students, a request for help to supervisors, or departmental administrators might prove fruitful.

Finally, although this is easy to say, since I am not in a low at the moment and I cannot, like the astrologers, predict what the future may bring - my own and others experiences suggest that the lows of doing a part-time PhD are inevitable, but temporary. They do pass, and despite the pressures we all feel when trying to deliver Mission Impossible, and give 200% to each of our commitments - work, family and the research, my view is that *yes, it is worth it after all.*

References

Malthouse, TJ, (1997) Childcare, Business and Social Change, Institute of Directors Employment Comment

Phillips, EM and Pugh, DS (1994) How to get a PhD, a Handbook for Students and their Supervisors, Open University Press, Buckingham

Silverman, D (2000) Doing Qualitative Research, A Practical Handbook, Sage, London

Tanton, M (1994) Women in Management, A Developing Presence, Routledge, London and New York

In Brief

- Juggling the various demands of my life was the main part-time difficulty.

- I maintained my enthusiasm by selecting a highly interesting and emotive topic.

- The value of peer networks can never be underestimated.

- 'Highs' and 'lows' can be intensified through part time study.

A PhD in Just Over a Year and a Half

Frank Waring
*Reading Geography for his Doctorate, Frank also works as a
Programme Administrator in a Research Institute.*

If you saw the title of this chapter on the front page of the *Times
Higher* would you think it was the latest marketing ploy put
forward by the Director of Postgraduate Studies at Borchester
University? Perhaps you would assume it heralded the
discovery by QAA auditors of lurid details concerning a dubious
franchise scheme in Ruritania by Ambridge University College.
Well no, it could simply be describing something altogether
more routine and generally accepted by the Harris Report on
postgraduate study, the Dearing Inquiry and the funding
councils. Almost certainly, it has been embodied in a QAA code
of practice somewhere. It is, of course, the 'standard' part-time
PhD.

This year many other enthusiasts like me will have registered for
part-time postgraduate study leading to a PhD. Each will be
confronting the time pressures of fitting a demanding
educational experience into all the other responsibilities they
have to partners, children, in-laws, work and leisure activities.
(Leisure activities? - come on, is this supposed to be a serious
article?) As part-time research students, they could be hoping to
complete their theses by 2004 – six calendar years of sustained
effort, but how much actual research and writing time?
Obviously, the figure will differ from student to student, but by
the definition of being part-time students, the period will be less
than the six calendar years of their fee-paying registration.

The Part-Time Calculation

OK, so my chapter heading was meant to get your attention, but
perhaps it is not quite such an off-the-wall concept as it may at
first seem. My by-line is based on a rather daunting calculation I

made in embarking upon my own part-time research in Medieval Landscape History. I consider myself lucky to be working part-time at the university at which I am studying, having my own office and ready access to the library, Web and GIS computing resources I need to undertake the project. Because of my partner's encouraging attitude, I have been able to take a part-time appointment and use some of the remaining time for research. In some ways, therefore, my calculation was based, if not on a best-case scenario, then at least on the advantages set out above. Since beginning the research, my respect for those I know who are undertaking part-time research while working full-time outside a university environment has grown immensely.

The Research Day and Time Factors

As a self-funding student, the calculation I am referring to concerns the time I can dedicate to research over the period that I am able to sustain the financial cost of the enterprise (about £8,000 in total over six years, based on 1999 fees). The unit of time currency I used in my calculation was 'the research day'. I haven't found any exchange rates for this listed by the Bank Of England, and rather like the medieval mark it should be treated as unit of account rather than hard currency. I defined my research day as a dedicated period of about 8-10 hours that I could guarantee to allocate to research activity. I decided that taking account of other responsibilities (work, family and home, cats and horse) and including time at the weekend, I could allocate 1½ research days per week to my PhD. Advice from my supervisors and the departmental postgraduate tutor indicated that I would need to decide on a working pattern as early as possible and be prepared to modify it as appropriate. I was informed that some part-time researchers work in bursts of concentrated effort, others on a more regular basis of so many hours per week. I settled on the latter approach.

My planning figures attempted to avoid what Phillips' and Pugh term as *'over-ambitious estimates of what they [students] could accomplish during the first year.'* The calculation was simple: assume 50 potential working weeks in the year (quite generous actually), multiply first by 1½ and then by 6. The result: 450 research days . . . less than a year and a half. I added some bonus time at weekends and in holiday periods (say, another 150 research days) for fieldwork and assumed that I would be doing some relevant reading most evenings in my first full-time-equivalent year. All this did not include any courses, conferences and induction seminars that my supervisors recommended, or that the department provided.

Two major questions presented themselves after this: was I going to be determined, motivated and organised enough to stick to my time estimate? Was the time I thought I had going to be enough to meet the requirements of the different components of research? Not very encouragingly, the honest answers at this stage are, respectively, 'I hope so' and 'I hope so'. Various demands competing for time include secondary source reading for the literature review; skill training and development; the evolution of a methodology; the identification of some theoretical foundations for the research; initial fieldwork and the preparation of a formal research proposal for purposes of review and upgrading. Here, at least, there are some clear advantages to part-time study. What you cannot timetable in from this year's faculty or university training programmes are likely to be available again next year (such naivety). I opted for an introductory course on Geographical Information Systems this year, but need to attend an undergraduate course on Latin palaeography run by one of my supervisors next year.

What emerged from my attempt to answer the two questions above was, in the words of Basil Fawlty, 'the bleedin' obvious'. In order to make the best use of available time, part-time researchers need to integrate a range of experiences (both work-based and academic). They need to look for beneficial links between apparently disparate activities. (Eg. writing short chapters for books and preparing for research tutorials.) And they need to stimulate more latent abilities (in my case, more effective multi-tasking). Only then will they stand a chance of squeezing the most out of whatever time they have available.

Part-Time Needs

However, it quickly occurred to me that this enabling, holistic, integrative ability is not an exclusive part-time research requirement. It is just as relevant to full-time researchers. I began to realise that there was an implicit assumption in my approach that part-time research postgraduates were somehow 'special' cases (head cases, perhaps, special cases, well maybe not). There seem to be two interwoven strands in trying to identify the particular support needs of part-time researchers. One strand concerns those issues that stem from the nature of the research process itself, whether full or part-time (e.g. intellectual capacity, skill development, academic writing ability, time management, etc.). Another strand concerns those areas in which part-time researchers face either different problems from full-time researchers, or more acute forms of common problems. I would suggest four such areas: accessing resources and facilities; research training; sustaining motivation and enthusiasm; and financing the process.

The accessibility of resources and facilities is a particular problem for part-time students. My experience so far has been positive in this context. Practical workshops on GIS techniques were run twice each week for a term, providing alternate times of access and easing the pressure on computer laboratory space, although this doubled the staff teaching commitment. Ironically, however, this approach was moulded into a popular undergraduate course from which postgraduates could benefit. The provision of a dedicated postgraduate computer room in the department, that is also accessible at weekends, has helped with revision of techniques and practical applications. Postgraduate tutorial timings are usually arranged around lunch periods and this certainly helps in managing work and study. Central resources cannot necessarily be as flexible. Weekend library facilities could still be improved for part-time students, (notably in terms of service provision for borrowing) though only at increased staff cost. On-line ordering, book renewal, bibliographic services and web access are certainly service enhancements that are appreciated by part-time students.

Research training for part-time postgraduates can be seen as a sub-set of the accessibility issues discussed above, and is a common issue for all postgraduates. However, the timing, format and support materials for skills training courses and modules can be particularly critical for part-time students. The factors that have to be taken into consideration include the relevance and quality of the training, given the limited amount of time available to part-timers. The availability and timing of the training in relation to its application; and the prioritisation of learning needs within the research process are also major factors.. Part-time students may take longer to attain a given skill level and may have to compromise in developing two skills sequentially, though both may ideally be needed simultaneously. In my case, for example, it would have been better to have developed the GIS and Latin palaeographic skills together rather than sequentially. However, talking to other part-time postgraduates has revealed several creative and 'self-help' alternatives to meeting learning needs. Peer-group tutoring and the identification of self-help manuals is invaluable.

The Part-Time Marathon

Almost by definition, part-time research students are likely to be highly motivated – initially. It boosted my confidence to know that I was organised enough to compile an accepted research application and that I was actually embarking upon a project I had been hoping to start for some years. I don't think I am being too cynical in wondering whether intellectual curiosity, interest in the subject matter and personal achievement will be enough to sustain my enthusiasm when I hit the inevitable blockages along the way. Once again, the greater length of time over which part-time researchers have to sustain their commitment and motivation is a key factor. Self-comparison with full-time postgraduates working in the same filed may not be helpful. Interestingly, I have already been comparing my progress unfavourably with those of a full-time colleague researching in a cognate area. I know that I shouldn't be at the same point for several more months, but affectively, I cannot help but get anxious. I am trying to tackle this issue by keeping a research diary to catalogue actual progress against planned objectives.

Financially, my research is likely to become a more critical issue later in the process. Initially the confidence boost of beginning the research has mitigated its very real financial drain on resources. I can see that the longer it goes on, the greater will be the personal and financial investment and losses made in the project. The relative lack of funding options for part-time research students is definitely an issue.

So what have I learned about the process of part-time research in the short time I have been registered so far?

Afterword

I have found that part-time research for a Doctorate is like no other educational experience I have had. It draws on such a wide range of skills and experience. It is intellectually and academically challenging and inspiringly motivating in its fundamental concept of creating knowledge. It is also a dauntingly forbidding journey towards independent academic judgement and self-reliance. In a more mundane sense, it is a self-imposed sentence of unremitting hard work for five or six years. It is already becoming part of my life – pervading most aspects of it and impinging on personal time and space. There is a clear need to re-appraise priorities and review accepted patterns of work and home life.

What do I hope to get out of it? In one sense it is a self-rewarding journey of discovery – I don't have any (well, not many) delusions about starting on an academic career at the age I will be when (if) I complete it. In another sense, however, the financial investment and the effort put in will mean that I will be keen to use the qualification as means of opening up employment opportunities within Higher Education.

If **you** are thinking of applying to start a PhD as a mature, part-time research student, my final piece of advice is to take as much time as you can (6 months or more) to think out what you actually want to do, how you want to do and how much it is going to cost. Then start to assemble resources (office space at home, an on-line computer etc.) and try to do some serious reading around the topic area that interests you. Finally, try to talk to some other people who have already proved their terminal madness by registering for some research.

Good luck...

102

Further Reading:

Becker, Howard S. (1986) *Writing for Social Scientists. How to start and finish your thesis, book or article.* Chicago: Chicago University Press.

Bell, Judith. (1987) *Doing Your Research Project.* Milton Keynes: Open University Press.

Cryer, Patricia. (1996) *The Research Student's Guide to Success.* Buckingham: Open University Press.

Cryer, Patricia (1997) *Handling Common Dilemmas in Supervision.* Buckingham: SRHE/THES

Phillips, Estelle M. and Pugh, D.S. (1994) *How to Get a Ph.D..2nd ed.* Milton Keynes: Open University Press.

Salmon, Phillida. (1992) *Achieving a PhD - ten students' experience.* Stoke-on-Trent: Trentham Books.

Other titles still available from the first series:

They always eat green apples: images of university and decisions at 16
Mike Heathfield and Nina Wakeford
ISBN: 0 901800 16 3   Type: Paperback   Price: £9.95

Juggling for a degree: *mature students' experience of university life*
Edited by Hilary Arksey, Ian Marchant and Cheryl Simmill
ISBN: 0 901800 49 X   Type: Paperback   Price: £9.95

How's your dissertation going: *students share the rough reality of dissertation and project work*
Liz Hampson
ISBN: 0 901800 51 1   Type: Paperback   Price: £9.95

In at the deep end: *first experiences of university teaching*
Edited by David Allan
ISBN: 0 901800 90 2   Type: Paperback   Price: £9.95

Beg, borrow or starve?: *how to finance your degree*
Anthony Hesketh
ISBN: 0 901800 99 6   Type: Paperback   Price: £9.95

Uneasy Chairs: *life as a professor*
Edited by Jeffrey Richards
ISBN: 1-86220-042-4   Type: Paperback   Price: £9.95

Take a Minute: *reflections on modern higher education administration*
Edited by Helena Thorley
ISBN: 1-86220-043-2   Type: Paperback   Price: £9.95

48 Warm-ups for group work
Edited by Jo Malseed
Type: Spiral bound   Price: £4.95

Titles in the Independent Studies Series:

How I got my first class degree:
Edited by Peter Tolmie
ISBN: **1-86220-092-0**   Type: Paperback   Price: £9.95

How I supported my son or daughter through University:
Edited by Lynne Boundy
ISBN: 0 901800 98 8   Type: Paperback   Price: £9.95

Also available through the School of Independent Studies:

Health Promoting Universities: *concept, experience and framework for action*
Edited by Agis D Tsouros, Gina Dowding, Jane Thompson, Mark Dooris
Published by World Health Organisation
ISBN 92 890 1285 4   Type: Paperback   Price: £20

Please note that all titles include P&P

For further information or to order any of the above titles please contact: Julie Rossall, School of Independent Studies, Lonsdale College, Lancaster University, Lancaster LA1 4YN.
Tel: 01524 593430   Fax: 01524 843934
Email: j.rossall@lancaster.ac.uk